Chart of
THE CLIPPER SHIP
SEA SERPENT
AROUND THE WORLD
1854–1855

# The

## *Sea Serpent*

# Journal

# The *Sea Serpent* Journal

Hugh McCulloch Gregory's
Voyage around the World in a Clipper Ship
1854–55

Edited by Robert H. Burgess

Published for The Mariners Museum
Newport News, Virginia
by the University Press of Virginia
Charlottesville

THE UNIVERSITY PRESS OF VIRGINIA

Copyright © 1975 by The Mariners Museum, Newport News, Virginia

First published 1975

Museum Publication Number 32


Library of Congress Cataloging in Publication Data
Gregory, Hugh McCulloch, 1834–1903.
   The Sea Serpent journal.
   (Museum publication no. 32)
   1.  Sea Serpent (Clipper Ship)  2.  Voyages around
the world.  I.  Burgess, Robert H., ed.  II.  Title.
III.  Mariners Museum, Newport News, Va.  Museum
publication no. 32. G440.S38G73  1975  910′.41  74–12382  ISBN 0–8139–0589–3

Printed in the United States of America

# *Preface*

On November 8, 1927, Charles T. Harbeck of Brooklyn, New York, wrote to the secretary-treasurer of the United States Naval Institute, Annapolis, Maryland, as follows: "In looking over some old matter the other day I came across a manuscript book in the form of a log or journal. . . . if you care to have it I shall be pleased to send it." Capt. H. A. Baldridge, then secretary-treasurer of the institute, wrote to Harbeck to accept the journal, and it was duly sent to the institute, where it reposed for the next forty-four years. On a research visit to The Mariners Museum in 1971, Lt. Comdr. (ret.) Arnold S. Lott, Editor (books) for the institute, mentioned the journal and offered it to the museum, which accepted it for its library.

The marbled hardboard covers, 9¾″ × 8″, bind 165 pages of light blue, faintly lined paper, 150 of which are filled with neat handwriting. The black ink has faded slightly, and the corners of the covers are chafed from wear. At one time the journal was secured with tape and red sealing wax, remnants of which adhere to the yellowed covers. The sealing was probably placed on the journal by the chronicler, whose last entry, on October 26, 1856, was: "Remember, this is a private journal."

The journal is the day-by-day account of a voyage in the clipper ship *Sea Serpent* from February 24, 1854, to February 16, 1855, around the world, from New York to New York by way of Cape Horn, San Francisco, Hong Kong, and Shanghai. It was written by twenty-year-old Hugh McCulloch Gregory, who was a seaman, or boy, on that voyage. He apparently enjoyed a somewhat privileged position. He may have secured his billet as a result of the influence of his father, a distinguished naval officer and friend of the clipper's master, Capt. William Howland. On one occasion, writes Gregory, the captain gave him an apple, and on others the two conversed about Gregory's father and other of their acquaintances. Also, Gregory was furnished the ship's daily position to record in his journal. Yet Gregory carried out his shipboard duties as any other seaman and never shirked duty.

Another passage in the *Sea Serpent* was described by Bayard Taylor, who sailed as passenger from Whampoa, China, to New York in September 1853. This account appeared in his *Visit to India, China and Japan in 1853,*" published in 1875 and cited in volume 2 of *American Clipper Ships, 1833–58,* by Octavius T. Howe and Frederick C. Matthews, in the section dealing with the *Sea Serpent*. Gregory sailed on the *Sea Serpent* on the voyage following Taylor's, and both mention some of the same officers of the ship. It is interesting to compare the two accounts, one written from the viewpoint of a passenger and the other from the viewpoint of a seaman. Taylor's is more descriptive of his surroundings. Gregory's, naturally, is concerned with the working of the ship, handling sail, etc.

In an attempt to learn more about Hugh McCulloch Gregory and the *Sea Serpent* a number of letters were sent to various museums, libraries, historical societies, government facilities, and individuals. What little light can be shed on this mariner and this ship has come from responses to some of these inquiries. David Hull, Librarian of the San Francisco Maritime Museum, went beyond the call of duty in searching for Gregory's death date and place of burial, both of which he did locate.

Others cooperating in this project were the California Historical Society, San Francisco; U.S. Naval Institute, Annapolis; Seamen's Bank for Savings, New York; Connecticut State Library, Hartford; Naval History Division, Department of the Navy, Washington, D.C.; Trinity College Library, Hartford; California State Library, Sacramento; Bergen Sjofartmuseum, Bergen, Norway; Connecticut Historical Society, Hartford; Mystic Seaport, Mystic, Connecticut; and the library of The Mariners Museum.

The volume *Ancestors and Descendants of Henry Gregory*, compiled and published in 1933 by Grant Gregory, Provincetown, Massachusetts, was a valuable source of information. The *Shipping Gazette Weekly Summary* afforded the means of tracing the last days of the *Sea Serpent*. Thanks are offered to Philip C. F. Smith, Managing Editor of the maritime history quarterly *American Neptune*, for inserting in that journal a plea for information about Hugh McCulloch Gregory.

Drawings of the course of the *Sea Serpent*'s voyage and that ship's sail plan were made by Clifford H. Hancock, Assistant to the Curator, Ships and Ship Models, The Mariners Museum. His assistance in this project is most appreciated. The late John F. Leavitt, marine artist and Associate Curator of Mystic Seaport, was most helpful in providing a sketch of the *Sea Serpent* from which the sail plan was developed.

In preparing the journal for publication, misspelled words have been corrected, numeration has been standardized, punctuation and abbreviations have been somewhat modernized, and italic type has been used rather than underlining. Errors in names of places and of ships, where possible to verify, have been corrected. Apart from these adjustments, this version of the journal reads the same as the one written by the young seaman Gregory.

# Contents

# Illustrations

England, and reported having passed the *Progress* on June 21 in latitude 47° N, longitude 37° W. At that time the vessel was waterlogged and abandoned, timber-laden and with two boats on the skids. The crew had left in the other boat, the report surmised, as she appeared to have carried three. Actually, the bark *Gulnare* had rescued the crew of seventeen from the disabled ship and had brought them into Northport, Nova Scotia.

When the steamer *Dresden* arrived in Weser, Germany, from Baltimore, she reported passing the derelict bark *Progress* on June 30 in latitude 40°26′ N, longitude 36°22′ W and added that "the wreck was in a very dangerous position for the navigation." The master of the steamer *Vesta*, arriving at Liverpool on August 14 from New Orleans, reported that on August 7, in latitude 46°20′ N, longitude 35°10′ W, he had passed the *Progress*. "Her main and mizzen topmasts were broken off a little above the eyes of the lower rigging; foremast, topmast and topgallant mast standing; a piece of topgallant yard and sail swinging about aloft; jibboom gone, also starboard anchor. After house all right, the earthen plate on house deck, the wheel broken and lying against port bulwark. Pine planks on deck, starboard bulwarks amidships gone. No life on board; vessel will apparently float for some considerable time."

As the derelict continued her eastward drift, the captain of the steamer *Eglantine* arrived at Londonderry from Philadelphia on August 31 and reported: "On August 22, latitude 46°17′ N, longitude 32°55′ W, passed ship *Progress*, abandoned and waterlogged, no boats on board, most of deck board complete. Very dangerous to navigation." It seems unbelievable that the forty-one-year-old vessel, after a strenuous career of beating around Cape Horn as the *Sea Serpent* and then as a timber drogher across the North Atlantic, could withstand the punishment of wallowing in midocean and being swept constantly by the heavy seas. But she went on.

The steamer *Trewellard* put in at Dunkirk on September 20 and reported having passed the *Progress* on September 10 in latitude 45°10′ N, longitude 31°30′ W. In Trinidad, by cable received on September 26, it was reported that the steamer *Strathesk* "boarded at sea in latitude 44° N, longitude 31° W, a derelict vessel which proved to be the Norwegian bark *Progress*. She was waterlogged and breaking up, and in a position dangerous to navigation." The next report of the clipper, from Leghorn, Italy, on September 30, was made by the steamer *Grip Fast*, from Labrador: "Passed the derelict bark *Progress*, of Holmestrand, on September 20 in 44° N, 29° W." Then in Havre, France, on October 8, the bark *Ardgowan*, from Astoria, logged the report: "Passed the derelict Norwegian bark *Progress* on September 27, in 45° N, 24° W." And that was the last report of a sighting of the derelict published in the *Shipping Gazette Weekly Summary*.

Derelict ships were a great hazard to shipping in the North Atlantic during the latter part of the nineteenth century. The topic was a popular one in maritime periodicals and was a cause of concern in the Hydrographic Office, Bureau of Navigation, Navy Department, Washington, D.C. In 1893 that office prepared a wreck chart on which were traced the movements of reported derelicts in the North Atlantic 1887–91 inclusive. The *Progress* appears on a list of derelicts accompanying the chart and is shown as having drifted 1,120 miles in ninety-three days and as having been reported nineteen times. The last such report, made to that unit on September 13, placed the wreck in latitude 44°18′ N, longitude 30°33′ W. (One sailing ship on that list, the three-masted schooner *Wyer G. Sargent*, had drifted 5,500 miles in 615 days and had been reported thirty-four times.)

*Nautical Magazine* for September 1899 carried an article entitled "Derelict Ships," which opened with the following paragraph:

Every gale of exceptional violence that vexes the waste of waters which separates, yet unites, the Old World and the New, leaves in its wake some abandoned sailing ships. As a general rule these unfortunate derelicts are built of wood. Their holds are tightly packed with timber, and a heavy deck-load adds to the risk of navigation. Often such ships have had a glorious past. After carrying costly cargoes to every part of the world, with renown to themselves and profit to their owners, old age finds them sold to Scandinavia and engaged in the North American timber trade. Under the influence of a careening cyclone the worn-out cargo-carrier meets her fate shudderingly. The savage sea opens wide the devoted vessel's straining seams, the clanking pumps no longer cope with the ever-increasing ingress of salt-sea water, and the weary crew are thankful to find safety on some stouter ship which happily heaves in sight. Thus a water-logged timber-laden vessel is left to drift deviously before every wind that flows, impelled hither and thither by the surface currents of old ocean, a menace to safe navigation, until the hull is riven asunder or reaches the shore.

Perhaps the *Sea Serpent* just disintegrated as her timber cargo worked loose in her hold. Or she may have caused the loss of another ship which ran afoul of her at night, ripping her bowels out on the waterlogged hulk. The clipper's end will never be known.

# Introduction

Research concerning the life of Hugh McCulloch Gregory has produced only a smattering of information. He was born in Brooklyn, New York, on December 14, 1834. A member of the class of 1856 at Trinity College, Hartford, Connecticut, he spent only his freshman year there. Perhaps he tired of his studies and as a result decided to go to sea. In his journal Gregory mentions having worked on board the *Great Republic* in 1853. At that time the clipper was in New York, preparing to depart on her maiden voyage to Liverpool. Gregory does not state whether he was working on board in loading the ship or as a member of the crew. The *Great Republic* burned at her dock on December 26, 1853. Once rebuilt, she did not get to sea until after Gregory had returned to New York on the *Sea Serpent* in 1855.

Gregory's activities immediately after his discharge from the *Sea Serpent* in 1855 are unknown. He eventually enlisted in the U.S. Navy and on May 27, 1861, was appointed acting master and ordered to duty on the U.S.S. *Patroon*, a wooden screw steamer 113 feet in length. On July 30, 1862, while commander of that vessel, he was placed in charge of the blockade of the St. Johns River, Florida. He was transferred to the 171-foot propeller steamer U.S.S. *Isaac Smith* later in 1862. On June 26, 1863, Gregory was assigned to command the U.S.S. *Honduras*, a 150-foot wooden sidewheel steamer. Early in July he was on patrol searching for the Confederate bark *Tacony* in the vicinity of Nova Scotia. On February 6, 1864, he resigned from the Navy. His name does not show up in the Civil War pension files, so apparently he did not apply for benefits.

Little is known of Gregory's activities following his naval service. In Lewis and Dryden's *Marine History of the Pacific Northwest*, edited by E. W. Wright and published in 1895 (reprint ed., 1967) there is the following notation:

Captain H. M. Gregory is one of the pioneer steamshipmen of the Coast, where he arrived forty years ago, and since that time has been on nearly all of its routes. He was for many years in the Pacific Mail and Holladay's employ, and has commanded several of the famous steamships of early days. When the *Shubrick* was sent north, with headquarters at Astoria, Captain Gregory was her master, and remained with her and her successor, the *Manzanita*, for several years. After leaving the lighthouse service he was captain of the steamers *Truckee* and *Homer* for a while, but at the present time is not actively employed.

Reference to the San Francisco city directory reveals that in 1894 Hugh M. Gregory was master of the steamer *Homer* and had an office at 109 East Street. In 1899 he was listed as a master mariner residing on Haight Street. He married twice but had no children. Register no. 8642 in the Office of Death Records at San Francisco's City Hall indicates that Gregory died on June 13, 1903, of cerebral apoplexy, at his home, 639 Haight Street, and that he was buried at the national cemetery. A check at the Presidio and Golden Gate national cemeteries reveals no listing of his burial. There was a national cemetery on Angel Island in 1903, but it was later moved, and the remains of those buried there were sent to various national cemeteries throughout the nation.

The *Sea Serpent*, an extreme clipper built by George Raynes at Portsmouth, New Hampshire, and launched in December 1850, measured 212 feet overall, 39.3 feet in beam, and 20.8 feet in depth of hold. Her owners were Grinnell, Minturn & Company of New York. The vessel's first three voyages were from New York to San Francisco, thence to Hong Kong and other ports in the Orient, and finally to New York. On her fourth voyage around the world Hugh McCulloch Gregory was a crew member. The *Sea Serpent* continued her lengthy voyages, varying her ports of call but usually making round-the-world passages. Renamed the *Progress*, she was sold in May 1874 by Grinnell, Minturn & Company to Chr. Christophersen, Norwegian consul in New York, for $19,000 and immediately thereafter was sold to Th. O. Olsen and others in Tønsberg, Norway. In 1883 the vessel was sold to Lorentz Rafen of Holmestrand for 48,000 Kr.

On June 12, 1891, bound from Quebec to Dublin with a cargo of deals, she was abandoned at sea in latitude 46° N, longitude 40° W.* On June 27 the steamer *Lord Londonderry* arrived at Avonmouth,

* The following reports of the drift of the *Progress* are from the *Shipping Gazette Weekly Summary* (London).

## "Our Mess"

## From New York to San Francisco

Starboard Watch:

Stephen Gurber

E. A. Glover

J. M. Glover

Harry Sickles

W. Clohecy

C. A. Bouton

Larboard Watch:

Tilghman Livingston

C. F. Koerner

E. Chichester

R. Clohecy

B. K. Burt

G. L. Packard

H. M. Gregory

Friday, February 24, 1854

The long-wished-for day has at last arrived. At 12 P.M. the towboat *Achilles* took us in tow and proceeded down the harbor. Off the Hook we parted company, and our voyage began. With our courses, topsails, topgallant sails and jibs, off we flew at the rate of 8 knots with a strong NW wind. At dusk, the mates chose their watches and, as luck had it, I was chosen by the 1st, Mr. Larrabee. At 8, turned in and slept till 12, when our watch (the port) went on deck till 4, when we again turned in for the rest of the night. As I stood on deck and scanned the horizon, I could tell where the city lay, by the hazy light that hung over it. The future now lies before me and God only knows when next I see home. Changes, too may happen there, but it is my prayer that the same faces that were there when I said Good-bye may be there to greet my return.

The wind thro' the night was variable and high, and the ship pitched about in high style, much to the discomfort of the unexperienced. Tho' green myself, I was not troubled at all, and tho' rather unsteady in my gait, still managed grandly.

Saturday, February 25.

Early this morning turned out and assisted in getting in on deck the two anchors and stowing the chains in the locker. I suffered very much from the cold, more I think than I ever did before. Iron is cold enough at any time, but on a cold, raw day it is most particularly so. And while I was freezing, there was Ned G., my chum, snoozing away as nice as could be. No land to be seen, but the blue water forms our only horizon. When and where I shall see the next land I know not. Several fellows seem to be victims to seasickness, and they look for all the world like walkable vinegar cruets, pretty well filled. Poor Burt, who knows the Captain's wife's sister, has been five or six times to the lee bulwarks and every time the ship pitches looks distressed. The Captain asked me whether I had been sick and, on a negative answer being given, said that I must have been born web-footed to have escaped where so many are sick. The wind, from N and W carried us on our way at the rate of 7½ knots. Two ships could be seen from the forecastle, one inward- and the other outward-bound, the latter being the *Michael Angelo*, most probably, as she sailed with us.

Sunday, February 26.

Crossed Gulf Stream. The wind freshening, in the forenoon furled flying jib and reefed topsails, and in the afternoon furled courses and spanker. Towards night, the wind increasing, took in everything but main topsail (close-reefed) and forestaysail. At 12 midnight the gale blew so that when the ship rolled, our lee yardarms were dipped. The sea was one mass of foam and the spray looked like living fire, with a phosphorescent light.

Monday, February 27.

At 3 in the morning the gale increased so that we were lee gunwale under several times. At this time a sea struck us and completely washed our decks, drenching me from head to foot. Towards morning it began to rain and the gale broke. At 11 A.M. set spanker, fore-, main and mizzen topsails, fore- and main courses and flying jib. While hoisting the main-topsail yard a sea struck us on our quarter which carried everything before it. I for one landed on a water cask to leeward and then was washed to windward, where I had the good luck to grab a rope and right myself. I was wet from head to foot and had even my boots full. Wind ESE and driving ahead 8½ knots per hour. Since crossing the Gulf Stream the weather has grown very much warmer. Another sea struck our room and flooded it completely, wetting my bunk and bedclothes. After shifting my clothes, while forward a sea came over our bows and and I got wet a second time. So I don't mean to put on any more dry clothes till we get to warm weather. Turned in all standing, wet as sop and oh! gracious how cold.

Tuesday, February 28.

At half past 7 set main spencer. Grumbled all night I was so cold on watch. Saw several gulls, or, as the sailors called them, right whale birds, hovering about. I wonder very much where they can manage to rest, for I have never seen them alight on our ship. In the afternoon saw a large bark to windward going on the same course as ourselves, but we soon passed ahead and left her by night out of sight. On watch from 8 to 12, the stars shone out bright and not a cloud could be seen. Wind from SE by E and speed 9½ knots. Lat. 37°2′ N.

Wednesday, March 1.

A total calm. Shook the reefs out of the fore-, main and mizzen top-sails and set fore-, main- and mizzen-topgallant sails and flying jib. Talking with Stephen today, he asked me if I knew Charles Downes, in California. He said that he was keeping a liquor store about 75 miles from Sacramento. In our morning watch coiled away all the hawsers. In our watch below took out all the chests and washed out our quarters. Took out my desk and looked at my daguerreotypes. It seemed almost as if I was home again among them. The sun was so strong that I put my bed and everything wet out to dry. A sailor's life after all is a pleasant one; it has its pleasures (loafing on the sunny side of a barrel) and its pains (a ducking on a cold day). SE by E. Lat. 35°43′ N.

Thursday, March 2.

During the night a breeze sprung up. At 6 set fore-, main and mizzen royals and then washed down decks. Saw a splendid rainbow astern; wonder if the sailor's adage will turn out right:

> A rainbow in the morning,
> Is a sailor's warning;
> A rainbow at night,
> Is a sailor's delight.

Went aloft for the first time and found no trouble at all. Set at 9 A.M. the fore-topsail studding sail and the starboard watch are busy getting the gear on the other yards. On my watch below washed my dirty clothes and hung them out to dry. In the afternoon saw a large ship to leeward and soon run her out of sight. The night was beautiful, the moon shining bright. As I walked the deck during my watch I could not but think (and a happy thought it was to me) that the same moon that shone on me likewise shone on those loved ones at home. Wind NW and going ahead 10 knots per hour.

Friday, March 3.

In the morning set main royal, fore-royal and foreyard studding-sails; stowed hawsers and spare running rigging. Amused myself in my watch below making a cravat ring. How at sea people do relish things that on shore they would not look at! Mush for breakfast, beans for dinner, and how I did help myself. Wind NW and steering a SE by E course at the rate of 11 knots per hour. Lat. 33°15′ N.

Saturday, March 4.

Wind slacking down, only going 6 knots. Hauled out my book of sums that I did at Corner's, and as I run over them my mind reverted to home and the room that they were done in. Found a sty beginning to appear in my right eye, and, tho' very sore, found very little sympathy on the part of my shipmates. Strange it is that sailors on shore are so noble-hearted and sympathize with everybody, while at sea an over sense of manliness seems to destroy every finer feeling. Hence if a man falls from aloft and by luck escapes with his life, it is made a jest of. Could not but admire the break of day. Long before the sun showed his fiery face, a faint glimmer of light began to glisten over the water, and it gradually grew lighter till the sun burst out. Hoisted on board, at 8 A.M., the lower fore studding sail and mended it, and then reset it. Saw a large ship to windward. Spent my watch below in writing and in teaching Ned Chichester navigation. Confound it! The ink bottle has fetched away followed by the oil bottle and a pretty mess our floor presents. At noon it was calm. Hoisted up the fore-topmast studding sail and topgallant studding sail. The weather was so warm today that I took off all my woolen clothes and felt quite comfortable; a most blessed change from New York climate. Began to write a letter to Mother. Lat. 31°18′ N. Took in towards night fore-topmast and -topgallant studding sails and and main-topmast and -topgallant staysails and fore-topmast staysail and jibs.

Sunday, March 5.

   A most beautiful day. All day we had no work and consequently had plenty of time to ourselves. Spent the morning in learning Mercator's sailing from the boatswain. Tried during the afternoon to get some sleep but, owing to the confounded fooling of the watch on deck, who would persist in talking and smoking in our room in spite of me, found it impossible. Found it so warm that I got out my straw hat. Had "duff" for dinner for the first time and as a change it was delightful, for, for the last week we have had "scouse," a miserable compound of crackers and salt beef made like hash and salt beef, nearly every day. Wind SW going 8 knots. The sea is as smooth as it is in Boston Harbor. Heard someone singing "Wait for the Wagon" and must say it awoke in my mind pleasant recollection of home. How often have I heard it sung by Miss Devens? And, too, I heard it sung by Eva and Anna just before I sailed. But ladies, pianos and singing are subjects not to be dwelt on in shipboard. For over ninety days more the ocean will form our horizon and the regular routine of ship duty engage our time, and then—San Francisco! Lat. 30°5′ N. Long. 43°11′ W.

Monday, March 6.

   Washed decks from 6 to 8 in the morning. While standing by the rail I suddenly felt a bucket descend on my devoted cranium, pretty much, as the Paddy thought, "like a thousand of bricks." Thinking nothing of it (tho' it pained me badly) I was looking over the rail; I felt something trickling down my face and to my amazement found it was blood. On an investigation found a severe cut in my head and, Charley Koerner going to the Captain, he sent for me and, after cutting the hair off, put a piece of court plaster on and said he thought it would soon get well. Stowed side ladder and reef jigs under the launch and got out studding sails, rolled them up and stowed them away under the after hatch. Also got out mizzen sail and repaired it between 2 and 4 P.M. Lat. 29°27′ N. Wind SE by E going 6½ knots. The Captain has most kindly promised to give me each day the latitude and longitude. Long. 42°50′ W. Distance run 147 miles. Course S 75 E.* At night furled main-topmast staysail.

Tuesday, March 7.

Two ships could just be seen to windward. While on the main crosstrees I could just see two white dots on the horizon which soon faded out of sight. The day was spent in putting up chafing gear and mending the crossjack, making sennit and foxes. A pretty sight my worthy roommates present. George Packard, or "Down East" as we call him, lies boots and all in his bunk reading a novel. He is a son of Professor P. of Bowdoin and knows Professor Goodwin, president of my "Alma Mater," very well. Bye the bye I wonder how all my friends at Trinity are? Charley K. lies also at full length with a pipe in his mouth reading *The Love Chase*, while Ned Chichester has followed his example with *The Hunchback*. A hopeful set we are! I have been studying *Middle Latitude Sailing* seated astraddle of "Chips" bench, and the Captain very kindly showed me. He is a true man, every inch of him, and I feel grateful to him for his many little attentions towards me. Whether he does it because he likes me or for "Auld Lang Syne's" sake, on Father's account, I know not, but must confess I hope it is the former. At dusk, as I was sitting on my chest reading, I heard the mate pass the order to the lookout to keep a sharp lookout to the leeward. On hurrying on deck I saw a large ship close on our lee bow, standing towards us. She soon passed astern and out of sight. Lat. 29°3′ N. Long. 39°27′ W. About 8 Ned Glover, Jack G., Charley K.,

* S ¾ E—*Ed.*

Ned C., and myself, having hooked a cabbage and some turnips, closed the door and had a feast. While preparing, the boatswain came in to ask some trivial question, ostensibly, but in reality to find out what was in the wind, I think, by his actions. It was no go, however, for everything was "stowed." Wind SSE going 6½ knots.

Wednesday, March 8.

Today has been a lazy one. Early in the morning the wind died away and left our sails flapping lazily against the masts. At noon clewed up main course, furled flying jib and outer jib and spanker. Spent most all day in making sennit, stowing and overhauling old sails and stowing hawsers. Somebody, evidently a "Black Baller," helped himself to my jackknife. I wish he would have done me the pleasure to have left it alone. Saw a "Portuguese man-of-war" quietly riding on the surface of the water. Lat. 28°56′ N.

Thursday, March 9.

From 2 to 4 this morning took the lee side of the wheel. During the morning and afternoon it was squally. At 10 A.M. furled the fore-, main and mizzen royals and mizzen-topgallant sail, and clewed up the fore-topgallant sail. Began to read in my watch below Goldsmith's poems, which I borrowed of Packard; and most beautiful did I find them. Poor Burt started to go aloft and after getting as far as the foretop began to get seasick and was obliged to come down. Poor fellow! I doubt if he will ever get over it, and fear he will have a hard time of it around the Horn. We are now in the track of the trade winds and will soon have the NE trade wind, which will last us till we get to 4° N, when we will have variables. Wind SE by E. Lat. 27°7′ N. Had "duff" for dinner, which, tho' hard as a brick, still is too great a luxury at sea to spurn. Heard one of the sailors expressing his ideas on religion, and queer ideas they were. He argued that Christ was not the Son of God, but was only styled so because by his purity of soul he was worthy to be called so, and I must say he was alone in his opinion, out of justice to the others. Queer it is that sailors who so often have death staring them in the face and whose lives are dependent upon the strength of man's work should be so reckless and free in their oaths. Yet so it is. Companionship, as it were, with danger renders them callous. Today we are thirteen days out of N.Y., and in seven days more we will probably reach the Line. At 5 P.M. set the mizzen-topgallant sail. Another squall struck us at 7 P.M., when all hands were called to shorten sail. Took in single reef in the fore- and main topsails, and then the watch went below. At 8 in the evening set main spencer. A most exciting scene is it when a squall strikes a ship. The men bustling about deck and the hurried orders of the mates conspire very much to mystify a greenhorn, while the "yo-heave-oos!" of the men as they hoist the yards and their regular tramp on deck fill up the scene. Speed 10 knots per hour.

Friday, March 10.

From 4 to 6 this morning had to take the lee wheel. It was not my turn but Burt's! Big fool, he has (confound it) a peculiar faculty of feeling so weak that he can't stand when his turn at the wheel comes, but wonderful to relate he is never weak when grub time comes. He is a regular "soldier," or shirk, and I had the exquisite pleasure to tell him of it. Next time I take his wheel I hope the sharks may eat me. And so I might say of several others, for when the order is given to "hold the reel" no one can be found. I can say for myself that I am no shirk, for tho' I sleep on a coil of rope on watch I am always on hand to execute an order. At 10 A.M., a squall arising, clewed up mizzen-topgallant sail and furled outer jib. Our old skipper seems determined to carry all sail till the last moment, for he says he will make a quick passage if there is such a thing in the calendar. Had a succession of squalls all day. At 4 A.M. sheeted home the mizzen-topgallant sail. A sail was seen on our weather quarter during the afternoon. Lat. 23°20′ N. Speed 10 knots. Wind SE by E. The forward part of the main deck and the forecastle were wet as could be, and I don't see how they managed to say she was a dry ship in N.Y. without a stretch of conscience. Beans for dinner! Much as I dislike them I was hungry enough to eat them. Poor Bouton expressed his opinion that he had no idea that he would have to work so hard at sea. He ought to have been on board the *Great Republic* and then he would talk different. At 11 at night it was discovered that a case of Vitriol had broken in the boatswain's locker, and the watch on deck were busy passing water and clearing out boxes, blocks, etc., so that the Vitriol could be got at.

Saturday, March 11.

When our watch turned out at 12 at night, we were kept passing water for about an hour when all danger was at an end. The morning was occupied in searching our chests and overhauling our clothes to see what damage the Vitriol had done. Some of the fellows had a great many clothes injured, for as a hole had been cut in the partition that separates the boy's room from the locker, all the Vitriol had run in on our floor and soaked into our chests. Luckily mine had a thick bottom and none leaked through. Was sick thro' the day, and the Captain gave me an opium pill and as I was turning away had the kindness to give me an apple. And a great luxury it was, for anything fresh is a luxury at sea. The starboard watch greased the royal masts down. Charley and I had to slush the trysail mast in the afternoon, and a dirty job it was. "Slush" is the refuse grease of the galley which is saved in a big barrel and is used for greasing the masts to make the yards hoist easily and to make ropes pliant. It is truly a vile compound, but one has to stick his hands in "like a gentleman," as Libby used to say. Lat. 20°2′ N. Long. 42°48′15″ W.

Sunday, March 12.

While washing decks from 6 to 8 in the morning, a ship hove in sight on the weather bow and about 7 A.M. was within a quarter of a mile of us. Showed our ensign and flag with our name on it and she showed hers. From all appearances she was a French whaler. I hope she will go into some American port and report us. Oh! how I longed to put a letter on board of her. She soon passed out of sight. Finished Goldsmith and began to read Burns. The Captain gave me chronometer time for working longitude, and I spent nearly all the morning studying on it and *Middle Latitude Sailing*, which I finished. Also wrote in a letter home and began one to Smith. Happy days have I spent so far at sea, and far happier do I anticipate. The sailors are beginning to talk about shaving us on the Line if we don't pay the forfeit, viz. $1. While watching the spray as it flew from our bows, I saw for the first time some flying fish. And little beauties were they as they skipped from wave to wave, their little bodies and wings gleaming in the sun. Lat. 16°7′ N. Long. 33°30′15″ W. During dog-watch I went up and sat on the foreyard. It was a most beautiful night and the wind, tho' fresh, was warm.

Monday, March 13.

At 1 o'clock this morning shook out the reef from the main topsail and set main royal. I loosed the royal, and, as it was my first time on the yard and it was dark and the ship pitching and rolling, I found it no easy job. At 8 A.M. the main-topmast and -topgallant staysails were set. About the same time a large bark was seen on our lee bow, standing to the N and W. While busy amidships, a puff of wind took my straw hat off and sent it flying overboard. I was very sorry as it was the only one I have and now we are in the tropics I have great need of it. At noon set the crossjack. Lat. 12°14′ N. Speed 11½ knots. Had a queer sort of a conversation with Bob in which he completely showed his character and self-conceit. He is but eighteen, and yet he informed me with the gravest face imaginable that Grinnell, Minturn & Co. begged him to go out as 3d mate of this ship, and that the next day the shipbuilder Brown offered to give him, after he had been one voyage in a sailing vessel, a 1st-mateship in one of the largest California steamers and in one year afterwards a captaincy of it. He says he was 3d engineer of a steamer running between San Francisco and Panama and afterwards of the *Independence,* which was wrecked. Now my private opinion is that he was in the first place nearer a waiter's berth than a 3d Engineer's, judging from his manners, and in the 2d place he was never offered anything more than a boy's berth by either G.M. & Co. or Brown. Spent most of the morning watch making "foxes." Had "spuds" for dinner, which is potatoes and pork; and a grand feast did I have, for "spuds" come but once a week.

Tuesday, March 14.

This morning at 4:30 set fore-topsail studding sail and at 7 A.M. the fore-topgallant studdingsail. At 3 P.M. set main-topsail studding sail. While washing decks one of the sailors found a flying fish lying on the main deck. It was about 7 inches long with wings about 4 inches in length and had very much the appearance of a smelt. Amused myself for a long while watching them as they started up on all sides of us; some of them would fly the length of the ship before they alighted. In the first dogwatch got my octant from the 1st mate. At 5 P.M. the outer jib was set. I got no pork for supper, owing to either the hoggishness of the boys in the forward room or the cheating of the cook, confounded Chinaman that he is. Lat. 8°5′ N. The wind has hauled more aft and shoves us ahead at the rate of 10 knots. The weather is very warm, almost uncomfortably so. While sitting on the topgallant forecastle one of the sailors named Harry, who has taken quite a fancy to me, came and offered to show me how to make all sorts of sailor knots. He seems to be a very fine man, much above the ordinary run of sailors, and seems to know his profession well.

Wednesday, March 15.

At 1:30 in the morning took in all the studding sails because they would not allow the ship to steer her course. From 2 to 4 my turn at the lee wheel, and "Jack the Jerseyman" let me go to windward and steer her myself. I flatter myself I managed very well for my first time. At 5 A.M. set fore-topmast and -topgallant studding sails and main-topgallant studding sail. In the morning all the watch with the exception of myself were busy setting up the bobstays and other head rigging. I, unlucky genius, was ordered to assist "Chips" in caulking the poop deck, and the job of fixing the pitch to pay the seams with fell to my lot. So I spent all the morning in the galley, melting pitch and also myself, quarreling with the cook and blessing (over the left) the heat, "Chips" and everything in general. Such a confounded jabbering in Chinese I never heard before and never wish to hear again. To add to my good nature? when I asked the cook for a drink of water, he gave me salt water, for which he narrowly escaped a thrashing by a precipitate retreat. Lat. 4°52′ N. The wind is light and the sun very powerful. The "old Harry" seems to have got among the pigs, for five times during the dogwatch from 6 to 8 in the evening did they make their appearance on deck, and as many times had the starboard watch to catch them. The evening was so very warm that Charley K. and myself went forward and took a bath, he pouring a couple of buckets over my head and I returning the favor. I never enjoyed a bath so much in my life. During our watch, between 10 and 12, Charley and I, on walking the deck, discovered that we were the only ones of the boys awake. Searching, we found Ned and Bob side by side asleep on a coil of rope to windward, and Burt on top the hurricane house. No time was lost in devising a trick to play on them, and it was agreed to lash Bob and Ned together and tie them to a belaying pin and to lash Burt's legs to the mainsail. Charley lashed Ned and Bob, and I, Burt, and then we went forward and let the pigs out, knowing well that the boatswain would call all the boys to put them in again. Letting them out, we came aft and laid down. Soon the pigs, some twenty in number, came grunting down the main deck, and the boatswain began to curse and swear at them and sung out for the boys. Such a scrabbling I never saw before. Bob and Ned went head over heels and Burt nearly stuck his head thro' the mainsail. A long chase was it before we got the "critters" in, but a merry one was it. I thought I should die of laughter.

### Thursday, March 16.

At 5 in the morning brailed the spencer and took in all the studding sails. At 1:30 lowered spanker and main-topmast and -topgallant staysails. Saw forty or fifty porpoises playing around the ship. During the morning it was cloudy and rainy. At 4 P.M. set the main staysails and fore-topmast and -topgallant studding sails. Saw a splendid rainbow during the afternoon. Lat. 3° 15′ N. We expected to have been on the Line this afternoon but owing to light winds during the last twenty-four hours have been disappointed. During the greater part of the day it has been calm. For the last week have seen no gulls. Thursday is "duff" day, and always 5 minutes before 8 bells a numerous array of tin pans can be seen hovering around the galley door. It rained hard during the night and all the empty water casks were filled.

### Friday, March 17.

Today has been very warm and variable, at one time a total calm and another a little breeze. However, calms predominated and for the last twenty-four hours we have made but 28 miles. In the morning George and I had to clean the quarter boat out and a disagreeable job it was, for the sun was very powerful and there was no shelter from its rays. At 1 A.M. took in all the studding sails and main-topgallant staysail. The Captain has been parading up and down the ship, whistling for a wind, but as yet there are no signs that his efforts will be successful. Stephen is at present regaling us with some of his choice observations, which are generally of so low a nature that I, for one, am totally disgusted with him and wish he would give his company to those who want it. The first thunder that I have heard, I heard today. Sold my smoking tobacco to Charley for $2, $1 more than I paid for it. The increase in price is owing to distance from land, a fact which wonderfully improves prices at sea, for sailors must have tobacco and, getting out of it, will pay any price for it. I shall be glad when we get thro' the variables, for it is decidedly provoking to be going at a slow rate, like we have for the last two or three days. Lat. 2°47′ N. The greater part of the night was very squally and "Stand by the royal halyards!" was repeated again and again. At 11 clewed up royals and furled outer jib. When I turned in at 12 I was so completely drenched that I had to shift everything.

Saturday, March 18.

It rained hard till 8 A.M., when it began to clear off. At 4, when our watch turned out, I was in hopes that as it rained so very hard the mate would allow us to keep under shelter, but alas! my hopes were soon frustrated by the mate singing out, "Stand by to pass water!" and out we all had to go. The rain fell in torrents and oil clothes were like paper before it. For over two hours we passed water, filling up all the water casks. When our watch went below I turned in. I was so chilled and tired and slept till 12. Then we boys had to slush down the royal and topgallant masts. I went up the main and must say I got enough of the job before I got thro'. By hanging on like Death I managed to slush not only the masts but also myself, almost as effectual as the Roman and Grecian athletes did in ancient times. No sooner had I reached the deck than the boatswain sent me up to slack the royal and topgallant buntlines. So up I had to go and, after perching myself on the topgallant yard, began my work. But no sooner would I slack a buntline than down it would fly and I had it to slack again. Finally I got mad, and if I didn't lash the whole of them so that it will be a job to unlash them, I hope I may be hanged. Our ship presents the appearance of a great washhouse, over one hundred and twenty articles of clothing hanging out to dry at the present moment. From every indication there is a bad storm to leeward of us. Lat. 1°35′ N. The wind is very light and we only average 4 knots per hour. At 5:30 furled royals.

Sunday, March 19.

At 2:30 set royals and outer jib. I loosed the fore-royal. At 5 in the morning clewed up royals, mainsail and crossjack. At breakfast the men made a regular assault on the cook because he was impudent, and the way kids, cups and hot coffee flew was a caution. The mate came forward and soon settled the dispute. About 9 A.M. saw lying about SE Saint Paul Island, which is in Lat. 0°55′ N. and Long. 29°22′ W. At 9:30 set main royal. Wind very light, almost a total calm. We are in Lat. 0°50′ N and, as I might almost say, in sight of the Line as it were. At noon set spanker, main-topmast staysail and studding sails. I hauled out my letters and wrote in them and likewise my daguerreotypes, one of which I opened for the first time since I left, and I almost imagined I saw the original before me, so striking a likeness is it. About 3 P.M. a light breeze sprang up and our prospects of crossing the Line tonight begin to brighten. A few days ago Charley K. and I had a quarrel and after high words we parted in anger. And moreover he keeps his place hereafter. If he knows not how to behave towards me as one gentleman should towards another, our acquaintance ends. He owes me an apology and have it I will before I have aught to say to him. Today he returned a note on the Captain for $5 which I had given him for teaching me navigation, and I canceled the bargain and destroyed it. About 6 or 7 this evening we crossed the Line and I may now say that I am a son of Neptune with truth, and privileged to play pranks off on the uninitiated. This time the sailors did nothing to us, which is generally the case when there are no passengers. At 8 set fore-royal. During the night took in all the studding sails.

Monday, March 20.

At 7 A.M. set mizzen royal, Burt going up to loose it. And such a balk as he made in getting up I never saw. After puffing and blowing worse than a porpoise he managed to get on the topgallant yard, and then, to the infinite amusement of all hands, he crawled over the forward part of the yard instead of going behind it as he ought to. About 10 A.M. set main-topgallant staysail. We had very light winds thro' the day and averaged but about 8 knots. Had several showers which to me at least were a perfect Godsend, for it was so intensely hot that anything in the shape of clouds and water was most acceptable. A shower at sea is a most beautiful sight, for long before it rains upon you, you can see it steadily advancing to windward, and after it passes over, you can trace its track far to leeward by rays of leaden hue falling from the clouds to the ocean. Have had a sore neck for several days and cannot imagine what produces it; unless it be sleeping in the open air. For the last week it has been so very hot that I have slept out on deck with my pea jacket thrown over me. Last night I was stowed away in a coil of rope, "wrapped in the arms of Morpheus," when a shower passed over us and, tho' it poured, nevertheless I slept on till Burt awoke me and informed me of the state of affairs, when I bolted for shelter. How at sea a person is obliged to be jack-of-all-trades, his own washerwoman, shoemaker etc. I could not but laugh at myself for the figure I must have cut, in washing my dirty clothes today. Had they seen me home they would have died with laughter, I verily believe. Got out my college album during the dogwatch, and as I read it, oh! how forcibly did it carry me back to old times and happy days spent in the companionship of those whose contributions are on its pages. Some of them (of the graduating class) I shall not see for years, but I believe even then our meeting will be as affectionate as our parting was, for a 𝛥𝛥 once is a 𝛥𝛥 forever. Lat. 0° 46′ S.

Tuesday, March 21.

This morning the SE trade winds struck us and we have been driving ahead at the rate of 10 knots. About noon a heavy squall struck us and the royals and crossjack were clewed up. Soon after, the mizzen royal ripped in two and, after being sent down and mended, was reset. At 4 P.M. the royals were set again. At 7 in the evening, another squall arising, the royals and jib topsail were furled. We have now very squally weather, tho' without much rain. All day I have been on the sick list, tho' doing duty. The sore on my neck has turned out to be a boil, and a very sore one too. It is right on the chord and makes my neck so sore that to move hurts me exceedingly. However my only resort is to do as the monkey did, "grin and bear it." Sympathy is wanting which softens every evil and which one gets so freely at home. I have been downhearted all day and were I at home would lay over for a day or two. However it's no go. Lat. 3° 24′ S. While at the wheel Knapp showed me the Southern Cross, which I have so often heard spoken of and so much longed to see. It strikes me that the stars south of the Line are not as bright as those north of it. The wind is steady and will carry us to 30° S, when we will again have variables. We make on an average over 3 degrees of latitude every twenty-four hours.

Wednesday, March 22.

Early this morning saw a most beautiful sight. Long before the moon set, the mass of dark clouds in the east began to rise and give way to the golden rays of the sun. Lighter and lighter it grew till the sun at last made its appearance, and then the sight was truly beautiful. All the dark clouds seemed fringed with gold, while here and there in an opening a flood of light streamed upwards. The more I see of my shipmates, the more my ideas of a sailor's chivalry and generosity vanish. All seem to be ruled by one law, "Each for himself and God for all," and a poor law is it. Made quite a bargain today. Promised my allowance of mush and rice for George's allowance of "duff." Our rice is poor stuff, being very wormy, and our mush is never cooked enough, so that all things considered I have driven a Yankee bargain. At 12 set royals. At 3 in the afternoon saw a large clipper ship standing NNW, evidently a guano ship, going into Havana for orders. She looked beautifully as she passed out of sight. Lat. 6°59′ S. Steering a SSW course, at the rate of 10½ knots. I must say I think the superstitious dread sailors have of sleeping with the moon's rays on their face is a humbug. They say that it draws one's face out of shape. Now tho' I have slept frequently so and love to lay watching it, I cannot discover, by the aid of a looking glass, that my face looks any the worse. At dusk saw a large brig to windward, homeward bound.

Thursday, March 23.

Had quite a row with old Billy about getting ahead of him when the coffee was served out. He threatened to pour his hot coffee over me and was wonderfully astonished when I told him if he did I would throw mine, pot and all, in his face. He went forward vowing vengeance and warning me to look out for my head some dark night. So I suspect he means to strike me with a reef point when we are reefing topsails. If he ever strikes me I will level him with a belaying pin. Lat. 10°43′ S. In the morning shifted the main braces. At noon the Captain had all those who had instruments up on the poop deck to take an altitude. The "old man" was very facetious and, talking about calms, said that he thought the only additional affliction Job needed to make him curse his Maker, was to go to sea and be becalmed on the Line. And I must say he spoke with a good deal of point, for a calm is very destructive to patience. Found in a book of travels a very pretty piece of poetry, viz:

> My soul is like the sea that cannot rest,
> And while my eyes their nightly vigils keep,
> Strange visions flit upon the deep blue wave—
> Visions that seem to tell of childhood's hours.
> The gale whistles thro' the shrouds the name of Mother;
> Blessed word! blessed thought! have I a Mother yet,
> That for her reckless sailor boy doth pray?
> Or have those silver locks, bowed down with care,
> Found in the grave that rest the holy share?

Going at the rate of 11 knots.

## Friday, March 24.

For the first time I missed my wheel on account of sickness. Job's comforters have begun again to persecute me, and I found myself so completely laid up that today I have been good for nothing. In the afternoon rove new forebraces. Lat. 14°25′ S. At 8 in the evening, a heavy squall arising, furled outer jib and royals. I got a drenching when I could least bear it, for I was very lame. A month out today and two more to come before our voyage is done.

## Saturday, March 25.

All the morning I had to pass water to wash the pump well out with. And, oh, God! how I suffered. Hardly able to crawl, I was made to carry and pump over 200 buckets of water. When I got done I was nearly crazy with pain. Perhaps I am too proud, but nevertheless I will go on with the ship's duties if I die for it, rather than ask for leave to go on the sick list. The officers know well enough how I suffer, and if they don't see fit to tell me, why there the matter shall rest. At noon set outer jib, main-topmast staysail and royals. Lat. 16°49′ S. At 6, furled royals. Went about twice during the night.

Sunday, March 26.

Today I did not turn out at all to do duty, because I was totally laid up, unable to move. I hated to do it, as a sick person is put down in the list of "soldiers," a name synonymous with laziness. At noon the watch was called to heave the lead. Bottom was found at 20 fathoms and from the dirt brought up we are on coral beds. All hands were immediately called to about ship and we were soon standing seaward. Dwight told me that we were, when we sounded, about 30 miles from Cape Frio, towards which a current was setting us. Saw astern, for the first time, one of Mother Carey's chickens, a small black bird with a white breast. I feel so much better that tonight I intend to go to work again when our watch turns out at 12. The wind for the last day or so has been light and today at 3 P.M. we were only going 6 knots, a sad falling off from the day's runs we have made since we crossed the Line. In the afternoon saw two sail on the lee bow, evidently schooners, and many were the surmises as to their character. Some said they were slavers; others, that they were fishermen or traders along the coast; tho' all agreed in one thing, that we must be very near land or we would not have seen such small craft. At 6 P.M. went about on larboard tack. At 8 furled mizzen-topgallant sail.

Monday, March 27.

In the morning set royals and mizzen-topgallant sail. I went on duty again, tho' still a little lame. At 3 P.M. furled main-topmast staysail. The wind has freshened and we now go 10 knots. Lat. 19°50′ S. At 3:30 P.M. spoke a large brig to windward. We made out her ensign (American) but were unable to make out what her name was. We showed ensign and private signal, both of which, by her lowering her flag a little and then hoisting it again, we knew she had made out. What a blessing to be reported at home it is, is only known to those who for weeks and weeks are most emphatically alone in the world. I myself feel 100 per cent happier since speaking the brig, because I know that those at home whom I love most, will know whereabouts I am and that I am safe so far on my journey, and that their anxiety will be relieved. And, too, it is pleasant to see anything at sea; it begets a social feeling, as it were, and gives a feeling to all that we are not alone, a feeling which grows imperceptibly on one when for day after day he sees naught but the blue water around and the blue sky over him. The crew, too, all seem to have brightened up and one thought animates all, "We shall be reported." I found in my portfolio two reminiscences of college, viz: a copy of the charges preferred against Wildman and an N.O. notice. What glorious old times did we Night-Owls have! Those were jolly hours we used to spend together in that lone wood by the river. At 4 P.M. set crossjack.

Tuesday, March 28.

The day began with heavy squalls of rain. Wind from the NW and ship steering SW by S, going at the rate of 14 knots! At 10 A.M., the wind having increased to a moderate gale, furled royals. At 11, furled topgallant sails; and at noon, the wind blowing a very heavy gale, all hands were called to shorten sail. The topsails were double-reefed and the outer jibs hauled down, the spanker reefed and the crossjack furled. At 2 P.M. took in jib, furled mainsail, and set the main spencer, the gale blowing very heavy. At 6 P.M., the gale beginning to break a little, set a reefed mainsail, and at 10 shook a reef out of the main topsail and set main-topgallant sail. Today for the first time I was aloft to reef. And exciting work it is; both wind and man seemed to rival each other in adding to the wildness of the scene, the former by its whistling thro' the rigging and the latter by yelling orders and "yo-heave-oos!" at the reef points. Lat. 23°24′ S.

Wednesday, March 29.

Early this morning I saw a most beautiful sight. It was Venus, just above the horizon, and a larger star I never saw, it almost giving as much light as the moon. The wind was still pretty high, yet not enough so to prevent setting sail again. At 7:30 A.M. shook reef out of fore-topsail, and set the fore- and mizzen-topgallant sails. At 11 A.M. shook the first reef out and set whole topsails. We were at work all the morning watch, setting up the fore-topmast backstays and mending the outer jib. Lat. 25°16′ S. At 3 P.M. shook the reef out of the spanker. Today I saw a great many stormy petrels, or Mother Carey's chickens, hovering about the ship. Had a wheel from 8 to 10 with Harry, a Norwegian who seems to have taken a great fancy to me, showing me how to do little sailorizing jobs and really I feel very grateful to him. He showed me Magellan's Clouds and Orion's belt.

Thursday, March 30.

At 7:30 P.M. set royals and jibs, the wind being very light. Saw a brig astern standing the same course as ourselves, S by W. At 9 A.M. sent down main course and bent a new one. We are now well off Rio and will soon be to the Horn, for which I have been most vigorously preparing today, having greased my boots and painted my oil clothes. Today I made out a bill of fare à la St. Nicholas:

| | |
|---|---|
| Sunday, Scouse—Duff— | Bread & Beef |
| Monday, Mush—Spuds— | " " |
| Tuesday, Scouse—Beans— | " " |
| Wednesday, Scouse—Rice— | " " |
| Thursday, Mush—Duff— | " " |
| Friday, Scouse—Beans— | " " |
| Saturday, Scouse—Cape Cod Turkey—" | " |

The scouse is a libel on pig fodder, the mush is never cooked, the beans are awful and the Cape Cod turkey, or in plain English, codfish, is the meanest mess of all. The coffee and tea, which we have morning and night, is a muddy compound not fit for any civilized man to drink. However I am always so hungry I can eat what is set before me without a second bidding. At 11 A.M. furled main spencer. Wind SSW. Lat. 26° 42′ S. In the middle watch hauled all the sails out of the after hatch to dry, rove new fore-topsail reef tackles, and made foxes. The days seem to pass like a dream to me, and I can hardly realize I have been from home over a month. George is distributing the pictures out of *Graham's Magazine* to the Chinese cooks, who are grinning from ear to ear with delight. The night was a beautiful one and the boatswain showed me where to find the Dog Star, Mars, Magellan's Clouds and altogether gave me quite an astronomical lecture.

Friday, March 31.

Today begins with light breezes. At 7 A.M. set royals. Course S ½ W; going 1½ knots per hour. Wind WSW. All the morning the watch were busy setting up main-topmast, -topgallant and -royal backstays. Saw a large black bird flying along the surface of the water, which the sailors told me was a whale bird. It had very much the appearance of a crow. Today's the last day of the month and we have been out thirty-five days. Lat. 27°12′ S. The 2d steward has just left the room, having been here for some time learning how to count in English. His name is Aiming and he seems to be very intelligent. I wrote numbers out for him as far as 20, with which he departed highly pleased. The port quarter boat was taken in on deck by the starboard watch early in the morning.

Saturday, April 1.

April fool's day. There was very little quizzing done, not a hundredth part of what I expected. For from the levity of sailors one would naturally suppose they would give their failing free scope on such a day. All day it was a total calm, not a ripple breaking the even surface of the water, and our ship floating like a log with the current. Lat. 27°19′ S, just 7 miles southing in twenty-four hours. The work went on in a listless manner and many a wish was expressed that we might have a double-reefed topsail breeze. One of our smart boys, Bob, let go the main-topgallant halyards, instead of crossjack brace which he was ordered to. The mate was very angry and gave it to him hot and heavy. From being so very smart, he walked forward looking rather small. Had a long talk with Dwight in the first night watch about New Haven, where he was at Yale.

Sunday, April 2.

Sunday and a beautiful day. A light NNE wind sprung up in the morning and the lower, topmast and topgallant fore studding sails were set at 7 A.M. and the main-topgallant studding sail, at 9 A.M. Mr. Dwight adjusted my octant for me at noon. At dinner a long discussion was started on the Bible, whether it was true or not. As one was an A. J. Davisite, a second rather inclined to infidelity, a third a Unitarian and myself an Episcopalian, of course no conclusion could be arrived at. So George and I proposed that as it was a sacred subject and we none of us L.L.D.s, we drop it and leave it to older heads to settle. So the matter ended. At 1 P.M. took in all the jibs. Lat. 27°36′ S. Course SW. At 4 P.M. set the lee lower and topmast fore studding sails. The breeze kept freshening, and as it arose so did the feelings of all. Everyone jumped to obey an order and all grumbling was stopped. Long. 39°31′ W.

Monday, April 3.

At 6 A.M. furled mizzen royal and settled down on topgallant halyards so as to allow the forward sails to draw better. At 8 A.M. took in lower and topmast fore studding sails and took in the swinging boom alongside (lee one). The sunrise today was particularly beautiful. Long before it became light the eastern horizon began to redden and gradually grow brighter and brighter till it was dazzling to behold. When the sun rose the clouds which lined the horizon were all tinged, as it were, with gold. Altogether it was the most beautiful sunrise I have seen as yet. The wind freshening, all the studding sails were taken in, and at 1:30 P.M. all hands were called to shorten sail. Royals and topgallant sails were furled and a single reef taken in mizzen topsail and double reef in fore- and main topsails. Rain fell in torrents for about four hours when it began to clear off and the wind to die down. After reefing topsails I was obliged to go below, having two more of Job's comforters, which pained me very much. At 9:30 shook a reef out of main topsail and set spanker. While setting the latter sail, the boom got loose from the socket and was with some difficulty got into its place again.

Tuesday, April 4.

At 1 in the morning the main-topgallant sail was set and at 3 the fore-topgallant sail. The boatswain came into our room looking for "soldiers" and, seeing me muffled up in a quilt, asleep on a chest, grabbed me. Mad at being routed out when it was known that I was on the sick list, I began to give him a regular lecture when he spoke and I found out who it was. I apologized and he cleared out, apparently little satisfied with his reception. At 8:30 A.M. the mizzen-topgallant sail was set. Not going on deck today, I improved the time and repacked my chest, putting my heavy clothes on top so as to be handy while going round the Horn. My instrument, Bowditch,* and nautical almanac Mr. Dwight took into his room, promising to take care of them for me. I also sold him my India rubber boots as they were so heavy I was afraid to go aloft in them and, tho' they would be

* Gregory is referring here to *The American Practical Navigator*, by Nathaniel Bowditch—*Ed.*

a great blessing on a rainy day, still I could not but think that safety came before comfort. The Captain has been talking to me, says he is sorry that I am so persecuted, and remarked that a young gentleman like me ought to write many a pretty thing in my journal. In the forenoon watch shook out the reefs in the main and mizzen topsails and set the outer jib and jib topsail; opened studdings sails and staysails to dry and sent down the topgallant studding sails on deck. The Captain had a fine double-barrel rifle out on the poop and fired several times at the boobies that were hovering about, nearly all of which were successful, proving the Captain to be a good shot. On the afternoon shook a reef out of the fore-topsail. At 3 P.M. loosed the royals and set them. Altitude of the sun at noon, 53°36′. Declination 5°43′ N. Lat. 30°29′ S. Long. 44°13′ W. The wind hauled to S by E and we were steering SW. At 4 P.M. set the crossjack.

## Wednesday, April 5.

At 5:30 A.M. set main-topgallant studding sails and, the wind hauling more aft, furled inner and outer jibs. At 6 A.M. set starboard lower and topmast fore studding sails. At 8 A.M. set port lower fore studding sail. A most beautiful day and warm, a circumstance I did not fail to improve by drying everything at all damp. Ned Chichester hauled out all his socks and proceeded grannylike to darn all holes therein. I could not but laugh to see how gravely he went to work, tho' sometimes when the yarn would part he would "darn" it in another sense. At 11 A.M. hauled down the port lower fore studding sail. Last night I dreamt I was home, and from thence my mind flew from one place to another among my friends. Suddenly a roll of the ship awoke me and I found myself, instead of at home, stretched at length on a chest. Bye the bye Ned vows that chest is "imitation pine" and, I think, poor at the best, for it is hard as a brick. Mr. Cornell a few days ago, in striking his dog, struck his hand against a locker, breaking a bone in one of his fingers. He is obliged to wear his arm in a sling. At 3 P.M. set main-topmast and -topgallant staysails and jib topsail. Spent most of the afternoon watch on the crossjack with the boatswain lashing new gaskets, for today I came off the sick list. Sun's Alt. 52°35′. Decl. 6°6′ N. Lat. 31°7′ S.

Thursday, April 6.

At 1:30 in the morning took in all the studding sails and at 4 A.M. furled fore- and mizzen royals and jib topsail. The wind was blowing lively from the NW and, the water being smooth, we were ploughing ahead at the rate of 12 knots an hour. At noon set fore-topmast studding sail but soon after took it in again. At 3 P.M. set fore- and mizzen royals and main spencer. Sun's Alt. 49°29′. Decl. 6°26′ N. Lat. 33°53′ S. The wind died away till midnight, when it breezed up again. At 12 brailed up main spencer.

Friday, April 7.

At 4 A.M. set inner and outer jibs and studding sails, which last, however, at 5, we hauled down again, the wind having hauled ahead to the SW. Took out, in my morning watch, my blankets, bed, etc., to dry, so as to have at least a dry "bunk" to turn into off the Horn. While overhauling my chest I found a great misfortune had befallen me, for I found that my daguerreotypes were beginning to fade, most probably from the action of the sea air. Saw a great many petrels and low latitude haglets, or whale birds. The petrel is all black with a white spot on its tail, instead of breast, as I thought. The haglet is as large as a crow, with a white breast, its back and wings gray, tipped with black. It is frequently seen sitting like a duck on the water, with wings expanded. This morning the sunrise was magnificent. Long before the sun rose, the eastern horizon was tinged with a red, almost blood red sky, while the sky above was a delicate pink. Soon these shades began to give way to a purple dazzling to look at, while as day dawned the pink gave way to a delicate blue. One solitary star alone shone, Venus, large and brilliant, so large indeed that one could not but compare it, in his mind, with the star that the shepherds so welcomed at Bethlehem. When the sun finally rose, his orb looked like a ball of fire, red, and then the effect was magnificent. Everything seemed bathed in a flood of red and purple, but soon alas! the dazzling colors subsided into the soberness of day, and one by one the clouds disappeared. During the morning watch furled main-topmast and -topgallant staysails. At 2:30 P.M. furled the crossjack and at 3, steering a SE ½ E course, went about on starboard tack, on a SW by S course. The wind freshening, at 3:30 furled fore-, main and mizzen royals and jib topsail. For the greater part of the morning and afternoon a large brig was in plain sight, evidently bound for Buenos Aires. While making a rush for the galley at supper, I slipped and fell full length. First thing I heard was "Come here, Mc, and I'll pick you up," and turning around saw the Captain standing near. I "vamoosed the ranche" immediately, feeling somehow or other a little flat.

Saturday, April 8.

At 12:30 this morning loosed and set royals. I loosed the main royal and, while tugging away at the bunt gasket, suddenly found the yard was being hoisted. Not relishing a ride and thinking that it was contrary to law to hoist a yard before sheeting home, I sung out, "Avast hoisting!" and, casting my gasket off, slid down to the topgallant yard, when the sail was sheeted home and hoisted. At 3:30 A.M. set main staysails and jib topsail. During the morning watch from 8 to 12 set fore-topmast and -topgallant and main-topgallant studding sails. Also cleaned the ship's cutlasses and muskets. The former are stamped "2nd Va. Reg." and are from their make of no recent date. What tales of bloodshed and death might they not unfold, could they but have the gift of speech! Unrove and shifted the lee fore-topsail brace and examined all the blocks on the main rigging to see whether they were secure. My chum Ned G. was guilty of a most ludicrous mistake, for, having been sent up to overhaul the mizzen-royal buntlines and stop them, what should he do but overhaul the clew line and stop it to the sheet. Of course when the royal was sheeted home this morning, great difficulty was experienced and the mate began to swear considerably about it. However the mistake was soon found out and remedied. The wind was light almost all day. Sun's Alt. 45°50'. Decl. 7°13' N. Lat. 36°45' S.

> I'm on the sea—I'm on the sea!
> I am where I would *ever* be,
> With the blue above and the blue below,
> And silence wheresoe'er I go.
> If a storm should come and awake the deep,
> What matter! I can ride and sleep! !

During the afternoon the fore and main studding sails were set and taken in again. At 10 it began to rain and rained the greater part of the night.

Sunday, April 9.

At 1 in the morning furled jib topsail and main staysails. While washing decks a ship hove in sight to windward, bearing right for us. At 7:30 A.M., still standing the same course, the Capt. ordered the main topsail to be hove aback. Gradually she neared us, the wind being light, and when about a mile distant, we saw her boat pulling for us. Soon after, the boat came to leeward and sooner than it takes to write it were her crew on deck. The Captain and 3d mate went aft while the men were speedily "Hail fellow, well met" with ours. One, a fine stalwart man, came into our quarters and, seating himself on a bench, soon had questions enough both to ask and to answer. He said his ship was the whaler *Corinthian*, Captain Stuart of New Bedford, thirty-eight months out and now homeward bound. Many a happy face there was at the tidings. Homeward bound and a chance to send letters! I did up for Mother a journal kept every Sunday, and also a letter for Smith, Hen Peck and Hen G., and gave them to him. Before long more than fifty letters for home were handed in. Finding they were short of tobacco and books, everyone who had either to spare produced it, and soon each had a bundle. I gave the one who took my letters all my chewing tobacco and magazines, and felt that even then I was but doing a slight return for the favor he was doing me. While he was talking I went to the side and examined the boat. The harpoons and lances were laying in a rack in the bows, ready for instant use, while the tub was standing athwartship with the line coiled away in Flemish coil. The Captain and 3d mate were loaded with little delicacies by the officers, which, of course, we forward could not give for the best reason in the world, viz: because we had not them. Our 2d mate furnished a file of newspapers, two boxes of figs, and some segars, while the Captain gave tobacco, beans and sundry little necessary things. About 11:30 A.M. the order was given to brace the main yard and the whalers' boat shoved off and pulled for their own craft, about 3 miles astern, which distance we had gained on her since morning, when she was within hail. A feeling of loneliness came over me as I saw her turn her head homeward, and I watched her till I could just see her topgallant masts on the horizon. They expected to reach home the first week in July and in that case my letters may reach home on the 4th. Another incident worthy of notice occurred today. We had fresh pork for dinner for the first time since we sailed, and a most agreeable feast it was, after living for a month and a half on salt provisions. Towards night the wind died away.

Monday, April 10.

At midnight a heavy squall came up from ahead. At 12:30 it blew so strong that we were obliged to furl royals, staysails, jib topsail, outer jib and topgallant sails, in fact all the light sails. While on the main-topgallant yard, "Sail ho!" cried the lookout. "Where away!" asked the Captain, who by this time had come on deck. "Broad on the weather beam!" "Ay! Ay! Show a light!" "Ay! Ay! sir." A light was shown, which we were convinced he saw, by his showing one in return. I watched the light till it disappeared in the gloom. At 3 A.M., the wind increasing to a gale, all hands were called to shorten sail. The fore- and main topsails were double-reefed and the crossjack furled. At 6 A.M., the wind slacking, a single reef was shaken out of the top-sails, and topgallant sails were set. The wind heading us off SE by E, we wore ship and stood W by S. In the forenoon watch set whole top-sails, jibs, unbent topgallant staysail, topgallant studding sails and sent down fore-topgallant-studding-sail booms. Sun's Alt. 42°51′. Decl. 7°59′ N. Lat. 38°58′ S. In the afternoon a strong breeze from SSW, steering W by S at the rate of 11 knots. Last night was the first time we have reefed topsails in the night. It was pitch dark, so dark that I could not see who was next to me on the yard, and every minute it would lighten so, that for a second a flood of light covered every object, and then darkness held its sway again. The wind increasing again, at 3 P.M. the fore- and mizzen-topgallant sails were furled. The last few days have given good proof of Maury's statement, viz: "that between 35° and 40° S was a dangerous part of the ocean, for a constant succession of squalls and calms required great care to be exercised in crossing it." We have had a most provoking series of calms generally followed by a gale or squall ever since we crossed 35° S. At 3:30 P.M. furled outer jib, and at 4, the wind increasing, all hands were again called to shorten sail; furled main-topgallant sail, double-reefed main topsail, single-reefed mizzen topsail, and double-reefed fore-topsail; hauled up the mainsail and while doing it one of the truss bolts broke and we were obliged to repair it during squall, after which we reset it.

Tuesday, April 11.

At 12 this morning set main-topgallant sail. Between 12 and 4 the
starboard watch shook a reef out of main topsail and mizzen topsail.
At 7:30 A.M. shook remaining reef out of main topsail and set outer
jib and mizzen-topgallant sail. The wind towards noon died away
and we almost totally becalmed; however, light breezes sprang up
during the rest of the day. At 4 P.M. shook reefs out of fore-topsail and
set fore and main royals. During all the afternoon watch we were
busy trying to fix main-topsail halyards. The gin was slewed by accident and caused the chain of the halyard to be full of turns so as to
hinder the yard from lowering or being hoisted, thereby endangering
the safety of the mast. The starboard watch set the fore-topgallant sail
during the early part of the afternoon. At 7 P.M. loosed crossjack and
mizzen royal and set them. Sun's Alt. 42°27′. Decl. 8°21′ N. Lat. 39° S.
Only 2 miles southing in twenty-four hours, a most provoking fact,
and one well calculated to try the patience of a saint. At that rate we
would not see the Horn for a month of Sundays. Last night was very
cold, and so was the day, for I was obliged to wear all my heavy cloth
clothes. The Captain went on a regular inspection today, going aloft
much more nimbly than one would suppose a man of his years could
do. All hands were busy today preparing for cold weather, greasing
boots, washing clothes, and sewing everything that needed mending.
We are on deep sea soundings, so the Captain says, as the difference in
the color of the water denotes, for here it is a deep, dirty green while
off soundings it is dark blue. He says we will be on soundings as far
as the Horn. Course SSW.


Wednesday, April 12.

During our morning watch unrove fore-topgallant braces and
shifted them end for end. Sun's Alt. 41°18′. Decl. 8°43′ N. Lat. 39°47′
S. Found among George's books Scott's *Guy Mannering*, which I immediately possessed myself of and read with the greatest pleasure. In
fact, a standard book is so rarely met with that when one is discovered,
more than a dozen claimants instantaneously present themselves.
There was very little done thro' the day, the starboard watch doing
nearly all that was done, cleaning halyard blocks and painting the
chain. I discovered quite a secret today, viz: that George is a nephew

of General Pierce's. He never says much about it, tho' one would naturally suppose that he would sometimes allude to it. At 5:30 P.M. furled crossjack. We made an arrangement with the boatswain about our watches, which could not fail to please all of us, viz: that all the watch but one might turn in, that one to rout them all out whenever an order was given. So after a long confab it was agreed that we should each stand watch for two hours. My watch fell from 8 to 10 and most agreeable to me was it, for the moon was at its full and hardly a cloud was to be seen. The weather too had moderated, so that I was not annoyed by the cold. Not a soul was on deck except the officers, the man at the wheel and the lookout, so that I had all the deck to leeward to myself, and a most glorious promenade did I have. I thought of home and endeavored to picture to my mind what each one was doing, wondering whether they were thinking of me, as I was of them. The latter part of my watch I spent talking to the boatswain, who bye the bye I think is a curious specimen. He unfolded to me, tho' a total stranger to him, a long tale of family troubles, which I would have endeavored to have kept to myself had I been in his case. He said his father failed in 1837, when the great money crash took place in N.Y., losing his all; and that from that time he became morose, and so embittered his family against him that they separated, scattering to the four winds of heaven; and that he had a number of letters from him, complaining of the desertion, which he had answered by desiring him to cease all intercourse with him. Now tho' this may be true, still it seems to me he ought not to be so free in his communications to total strangers (for I find he has told the same yarn to others). Steering SSW.

Thursday, April 13.

At 1 o'clock set jib topsail. For the last day or so I have been Jimmy Ducks, a title which I by no means relish. Jimmy Ducks is the title given to the one who feeds the chickens and pigs. And a most unruly set of subjects are pigs to feed, for when you come within sound of them such a squealing as is set up I never heard equalled by anything ashore. And as my patience never was very great, they generally end by not only getting their corn but also the bucket over their heads. The only emolument belonging to the office is the privilege of hooking fresh water enough to wash in, providing the mate doesn't catch you.

Many a time have I wished that I had but a swallow of water that I have thrown away at home because it wasn't cool enough. Sometimes our water is almost lukewarm, and it always has that peculiar taste which water will have that has stood for any length of time in a wooden receptacle. Then it is that I long for ice, but tho' I cry "Ice! Ice!" there is no ice. During the afternoon watch, unrove the spanker peak halyards. While cleaning the wheel the Captain came up and opened quite a conversation with me, giving me a description of Major McCulloch, who he said was a jolly man with a belly as big as a water cask. He said the last time he ever saw him was at the Astor House. One day when he came down to breakfast he saw to his astonishment McC. setting at the table. Asking him where he came from, McC. answered, he had come over in the steamer to drink a glass of wine with Gregory. He never saw him afterwards. He was very much pleased at the idea of my being a sophomore and remarked he thought it was more likely "ask for more" in my case. I never saw him so communicative before. I saw a large albatross sitting like a duck on the surface of the water. At 3:30 P.M. set crossjack. Long. 58° 11′ W. Sun's Alt. 40° 14′. Decl. 9° 5′ N. Lat. 40° 29′ S. Light winds during the day, steering S ½ W at the rate of 4 knots an hour. At 4 P.M. set lower and topmast fore, and main-topgallant studding sails.

Friday, April 14.

At 12:30 this morning set main spencer and took in lower fore studding sail. The wind increased, and we were going 11½ knots when the log was hove. At 8 A.M. set lower fore studding sail, and at 1 P.M. took in main-topgallant studding sail. During the morning took in and stowed away all the gear belonging to the swinging booms. Tho' cloudy during the early part of the day, at noon it cleared off and the wind slacked. Wind NW, steering S ½ W. Sun's Alt. 37° 6′. Decl. 9° 27′ N. Lat. 43° 15′ S. At 2:40 P.M. clewed up crossjack, brailed up main spencer and furled main-topgallant staysail. Towards night took up all the studding sails. The dew was very heavy thro' the night, and towards midnight it began to cloud up and grow foggy.

Saturday, April 15.

At 12:30 this morning furled royals and jib topsail, and at 8 A.M. set them again. At 11:30 A.M. set lower fore studding sail and at 4

P.M., main-topgallant studding sails. Our watch had to "slush" down, the mainmast falling to me. The spencer gaff, which I slushed for the first time today, gave me the only trouble I had, for the roll of the ship made it hard work to hang on. However, by dint of hanging on to the outhaul with one hand, I managed to slush it thoroughly with the other. Sun's Alt. 36°. Decl. 9°48′ N. Lat. 44° S. During the early part of the evening furled mizzen royal and took in all the studding sails. The wind was light thro' the day, and at night it began to rain. At 5 P.M. set main-topmast staysail.

Sunday, April 16.

A wet and foggy day. At 10 A.M. set lower and topmast fore and main-topgallant studding sails. While walking forward with Harry, I saw for the first time a Cape pigeon. It was about the size of a common pigeon, white breast, black head, with the back and wings alternately striped with white and black. A number of porpoises were playing around the ship all the morning, jumping their whole length out of water very often. Having nothing else to do, I broke into my trunk and got out all my mittens and other necessary articles for the Horn, for there is every prospect that we have very little clear weather till we get the other side. The wind hauled dead aft towards noon, and set the crossjack. But all the afternoon easterly winds prevailed and we had to brace sharp up. Should it hold as it is, a week would bring us to the long-desired-for haven. George has hauled out a silver watch and is trying to drive a bargain with the cook for it. A pretty mess our room presents, and one, too, well calculated to take all the romance from a sea life. Six of us huddled away in our little room, the majority in their bunks (some two in a bunk) and the rest writing and sewing. A water cask blocks up our window, and wet clothes and a dirty floor add to our comfort. The owners of the ship ought to be ashamed of themselves for the manner in which they have packed us boys in like pigs. And too, the ship is poorly found, a circumstance for which there is no excuse. There is no wonder that G.M. & Co. can afford to give to expeditions in search of Franklin and humane objects ashore and get a name for generosity, when they "gouge" so from the sailors in their employ.* At 8 P.M. set main spencer and took in studding sails. Lat.

---

* Gregory is referring here to the Grinnell expedition in search of Sir John Franklin, who, with a crew of more than 125 officers and men, had sailed to the Arctic in 1845

45°42′ S. Long. 61°30′ W. A cold and blustering night, going at the rate of 12 knots. I never suffered so from cold as I did when at the wheel.

Monday, April 17.

A sad, sad day, and one which to my dying day I shall never forget. At 6 A.M. set mizzen royal. At 7, the wind increasing to a gale, the royals were clewed up and orders given to lay aloft and furl them. Tilly and George sprang up the mizzen, when just as Tilly got onto the yard he slipped and fell, going overboard. "All hands! Man overboard!" spread like wildfire. Tacks and sheets were let fly, and every man went to work with a will. The royals, topgallant sails, jibs and main course and cross jack were furled, and all the topsails double-reefed. The ship was then wore and we stood back in hopes to save him, but alas! tho' many an anxious eye scanned the horizon, still no vestige of him could be seen, and with sad hearts we again stood on our way. Poor Tilly was a favorite with all hands, forward and aft. Of one of the first families in the country, he was a gentleman both by birth and education. George said the first he heard was a shriek and, looking, saw to his horror Tilly falling; he struck the spanker gaff and then, falling inboard, went like a shot thro' the foot of the spanker, falling overboard. Charley Koerner, who was at the wheel, says he saw him for a second ere he passed out of sight, and that he cried "Help! Help!" or something to that effect. Everything was done that man could do to save him; the Captain, at the first alarm throwing a life buoy over, but, going as we were 12 knots an hour, long before it touched the water he was out of sight. There were many different opinions about his fate, but by far the most merciful one is that he died before he struck the water. A heavy sea and a drizzling sleet made it extremely dangerous aloft; in fact, several of us boys came near going to our last home. I, for one, immediately after Tilly's death, was sent aloft to furl the lee yardarm of the fore-topgallant sail and a sorry job

---

in hope of finding the Northwest Passage. Henry Grinnell, wealthy New York merchant, philanthropist, and apparently part owner of the *Sea Serpent*, financed the first Grinnell expedition (1850–51). A second Grinnell expedition (1853–55) was dispatched to Arctic waters in a continued search for Franklin. A later search party established that Franklin's ships had been frozen in the ice in 1847 and that the survivors had headed south over land in 1848. None is known to have survived—*Ed.*

it was. Looking down I could see the ship rise on the crest of a huge wave, and then as she sank a dizziness seemed to overpower me and everything would seem to glide from under me. However I finished my work and, when I reached the deck, felt relieved. Jack Glover had a narrow escape, the sail throwing the footrope from under him, but, grasping at the sail, he clutched it and righted himself. For a second he thought he was lost. While bracing the main yard around, the outrigger snapped short off and fell on deck with a tremendous crash. Luckily no one was near it. At 2 P.M. set reefed mainsail and at 4, reefed spanker and inner jib. At dusk saw a brig to leeward, standing the same course as ourselves. A most gloomy evening did we fellows pass; for the reflection kept forcing itself on our minds that Tilly, the life and soul of our party, with whom in the morning we had cracked our jokes, was no more and that God only knew who next would follow. The thought too was disheartening, one of our number cut off without a moment's warning and to die such a death. All hands felt alike, old sailors wiping the tears from their eyes while the Captain and mate cried outright for a few seconds on the poop. But sadder tears will be shed over him by those at home, who will receive when least they expect it the sad tidings. Poor fellow! The howling winds and the roaring waters were his only requiem, and what ones more accordant with his profession? His memory will be cherished in the hearts of his shipmates. But enough. During the afternoon sent down main-topgallant-studding sail booms. At 8 P.M. pumped ship, pitch dark, rolling and pitching about at a great rate. When we held the reel,* the Captain came to George and asked several questions about poor Tilly, whether he thought he tried to swim, etc. He seemed to feel very bad, indeed. Between 8 and 12 the starboard watch shook a reef out of mainsail and set main topsail. Poor Jim, Tilly's chum, has been walking the deck nearly all day, sadly altered by grief, looking as pale and careworn as if he had had a fit of sickness. I never saw any man so altered in so short a space of time as him.

Tuesday, April 18.

   At 12 our watch shook reef out of fore- and mizzen topsails and set fore- and main-topgallant sails. At 2 A.M. shook reef out of mizzen

   * A log chip extended on a line from a wooden reel was streamed astern to determine the ship's speed—*Ed.*

topsail and set topgallant sail and crossjack. At 3 A.M. shook reef out of main topsail and set the royal. At 5 A.M. shook the reef out of fore-topsail and set outer jib and main-topmast staysail. At 8 A.M. sent down fore- and mizzen royals and unbent jib topsail. Course SSE, wind ENE, going at the rate of 9 knots. The day being very cold, nothing was done till 4 P.M., when the main royal was sent down. Stowed the royals, jib topsail and studding sails in the after hatch. The royal yards were lashed on the main deck, starboard side. I am mighty glad they were sent down, for it is no fool of a job to lay aloft in icy cold weather to furl royals. A universal gloom seems to be cast over the ship's company, very little singing or laughing being heard, all missing Tilly. Where for months a few men are to find their society from one another's company, the loss of one is more severely felt by the remainder than shore people would suppose. At 5 P.M. furled main-topmast staysail.

Wednesday, April 19.

A cold blustering day. At 6:30 A.M. set reefed spanker and at 7, the wind increasing, furled fore- and mizzen-topgallant sails and cross-jack. The rigging was covered with sleet and I literally thought I should freeze. Altered our course from S to SE by S so as to go outside of the Falkland Islands. Most of the boys are busy fishing for birds off the stern, of which there are any quantity, comprising albatross, Cape pigeons and Horn pigeons, the latter of which are pure white. For the first time the mate let us off from washing decks, a circumstance I for one was most thankful. At 1 P.M. called all hands and wore ship, going on larboard tack, steering WSW. The boatswain said he thought we would be a long time off the Cape, from all present indications. The starboard watch reefed mizzen topsail and furled outer jib. I begin to feel less and less like writing as the weather grows colder, but still, as I have begun, will finish my journal, tho' I hurry thro' and tumble into my bunk, glad to get all the warmth I can. Cold as it is, the Captain with his gun and the mate with a huge horse pistol are on the poop, firing at pigeons, a cold amusement. At 3 P.M. furled main-topgallant sail and at 4:30 called all hands to shorten sail, the wind increasing; double-reefed fore- and main topsails and furled mainsail. At 5 set main spencer. Between 8 and 12 the starboard watch set reefed mainsail.

Thursday, April 20.

At 4 A.M. set main-topgallant sail, shook a reef out of main topsail and brailed up main spencer. Between 4 and 8 A.M. the starboard watch set whole topsails, fore- and mizzen-topgallant sails, whole spanker and outer jib. During the early part of the morning tacked ship, standing SE on starboard tack. Got an observation at noon. Sun's Alt. 24°25′. Decl. 11°34′ N. Lat. 53°50′ S. Long. 65°07′ W. Direct distance from Cape Horn, 150 miles. At 4 P.M., it blowing strong, called all hands to shorten sail, furled fore- and mizzen-topgallant sails, and single-reefed fore- and main topsails. At 4:30 P.M. the watch on deck took a single reef in the mizzen topsail. Staten Island was in sight all the afternoon, looming up from the horizon like a huge bank of clouds, here and there a bright spot showing where some snow-capped cliff raised its high head to heaven. The sun, too, set in matchless splendor, casting its golden rays on the land, adding to the beauty of the scene. An opening betrayed where the Straits of La Maire lay, where we would go thro' if we could, but head winds prevent. Thro' the whole night watched terra firma with the greatest interest, at one time being within 5 miles of it. At 11:30 furled main-topgallant sail and outer jib.

Friday, April 21.

At 6 A.M. loosed main- and fore-topgallant sails and outer jib and set them. At 10 A.M. furled fore-topgallant sail and outer jib and at 2:30 P.M., main-topgallant sail. Weather icy cold and a tremendous heavy sea. At 4 P.M. called all hands and wore ship, heading SE by S at the time, standing on larboard tack, steering W by S. At 5 P.M. set main spencer. During the afternoon saw a large bark standing the same course as ourselves but were unable to signalize her.

Saturday, April 22.

At 5 A.M. set all three topgallant sails and brailed up main spencer. At 10 A.M. shook reef out of mizzen topsail and set outer jib. During the morning sent down the fore-topmast-studding-sail booms. At the beginning of the morning watch went about on starboard tack, standing SE. Land could be seen all day astern of us except when squalls intercepted the view. Snow fell several times and the weather was very cold. If we cannot get into the Pacific, I can truly say I have seen it, for, the weather clearing up, the Straits of La Maire were in broad view, opening from sea to sea affording a clear passage thro'. Flocks of Cape pigeons hovered around us all day while porpoises played around our bows, jumping from wave to wave. The swell was heavy and the ship labored heavily. The thermometer was 33°, a sufficient indication of the state of the weather. At 5 P.M. set main spencer, single-reefed mizzen topsail and furled fore- and mizzen-topgallant sails and outer jib. At 8, stood WSW on larboard tack.

Sunday, April 23.

At daylight set topgallant sails and outer jib and shook the reef out of mizzen topsail. At 8 A.M. called all hands and went about on starboard tack, steering SE by S. Cape Horn was in plain sight, with its snowy cliffs, while 3 points on our weather bow* were several large islands, looming up black and gloomy against the horizon. A large ship was in sight to leeward, bound the same way as ourselves. At noon went about again on larboard tack, steering W by S. At 1 P.M. brailed up main spencer. The thermometer stood at 34° above zero, a little warmer than yesterday, tho' sufficiently cold for my comfort. At 5 P.M. went about on starboard tack, steering S. Baffling winds and a strong current kept setting us in shore. During the night the starboard watch shook all reefs out and set whole topsails. Going into the forecastle during the evening, I found Dutch John reading the Bible to quite a little audience of his messmates. And a more attentive audience I never saw, the greatest reverence being exhibited by all, even by some from whom one would expect anything else.

Monday, April 24.

A most lovely morning, the sun shining bright and warm. The Horn, about 10 miles distant, and the adjacent isles formed a most striking picture. A solemn gray, such as one often reads about in the painted language of romance, cast its gloomy tints over the cliffs, which as day drew on gave way to shades of blue. A large bark lay to windward of us. There was very little breeze and the sea was smooth.

* An estimated relative bearing of an object in relation to the ship's fore-and-aft line, zero being directly ahead—*Ed.*

The ship was surrounded by albatross, gooneys, shags, and Cape pigeons, for the latter of which we boys were busy fishing all the morning, tho' with indifferent success, only catching one. At 11 A.M. set the crossjack and main-topmast staysail. All the afternoon kept slowly gaining on the bark, until at 5 P.M. we were directly abreast of him. He hoisted English colors and hailed us, "Ship ahoy!" "Hilloa!" "What ship is that?" "*Sea Serpent*, Howland, fifty-nine days out, bound from N.Y. to San Francisco, what bark is that?" *Niagara*, fifty days out from London, bound to Callao, been becalmed off Staten Island for a week, saw a large clipper in latitude 45° crossing royals, expect a blow from the NW!" was a lengthy reply returned. After a mutual desire to be reported had been expressed we began gradually to pass him. When about 2 miles astern we could see he was reefing topsails, evidently getting all snug for the night. He evidently told a broad lie when he said fifty days out, for from the build of the craft it was impossible she could sail the distance from London to Cape Horn in that number of days. At 6 P.M. single-reefed fore- and mizzen topsails, furled crossjack, mizzen-topgallant sail, main-topmast staysail and outer jib.

Tuesday, April 25.

Wind from the east all night, and at 1 A.M. passed the pitch of the Cape, steering a SW by S course. At 5 A.M. shook the reef out of mizzen topsail and set topgallant sail. At daylight the land was nowhere to be seen, and all hands congratulated themselves that they were in the Pacific and around the Horn, where we laid a little over two days and fairly on the last third of the voyage. The bragging Englishman, too, was nowhere to be seen, tho' we looked everywhere for him. About 7 A.M. land was seen off our lee bow, which proved to be the Islands of Diego Ramírez in Lat. 56°29′ S, Long. 68°43′ W. At 8 A.M. shook reef out of fore-topsail and set outer jib. The day was hazy and disagreeable and all my watch below I spent in my bunk, as the warmest and most comfortable place I could find. At 4 P.M. the island was out of sight and, the wind holding from the E, we altered our course to WSW, going at the rate of 8 knots per hour. At 7 P.M. the crossjack and main spencer were set by our watch, and an hour later the former was clewed up and the latter, brailed up by the starboard watch. Talking with the boatswain about our passage around the Horn, he said that "I might go around it 100 times and never see such luck as we have had this time." So far we have not had a single gale of wind, and our decks have never been wet since we made Staten Island except when we washed them down. Hurrah! for luck, I say. What strange changes one sees in the journey of life. While at school studying geography, I used to wonder what sort of a looking place Patagonia was and would have hooted at the idea had anyone told me that I should see it and pass around the Horn into the Pacific. And, yet here I am, having done it all, tho' I can hardly realize it.

### Wednesday, April 26.

Fresh breezes from the NE driving us thro' the water at the rate of 13 knots per hour on a WNW course. Early in the morning sent up the starboard fore-topmast-studding-sail boom, but as there were signs of a heavy blow we sent it down again. At 11:30 A.M. the wind suddenly chopped around to NNW and headed us off to W by N course. As the day began to end the wind began to increase. At 8 P.M. all hands were called to shorten sail; took in topgallant sails, outer jib; double-reefed fore- and main topsails and single-reefed mizzen topsail and set main spencer. It was raining in torrents and the tempest was howling at a fearful rate, and therefore it took no short time to take in the above-named sail and we were all chilled thro'. Grog was then served out and the watch went below. At 10 P.M. took in inner jib and reefed mainsail, after which we furled it. At 12 set reefed mainsail.

### Thursday, April 27.

The wind was still blowing fresh from the NW, which compelled us to steer a W by S course close-hauled. A sail was in sight on our lee bow, tho' too far off to make out her size, course or sail set. The wind still increasing, at 1 P.M. all hands were called to shorten sail; close-reefed topsails, furled mainsail and spanker. At 2 P.M. wore ship, wind WSW, and stood NNW. At 2:30 furled foresail and mizzen topsail. The gale was now awful, the sea one mass of foam and our decks wet and slippery. At 8 P.M., the wind lulling a little, set reefed foresail and close-reefed mizzen topsail. All night long the howling of the wind continued and the ship labored heavily, sometimes quivering from stem to stern when a huge wave would strike her. The sea ran very high and all forward was flooded as wave after wave came over her bows. Our Cape Horn seems to have begun now in real earnest.

Friday, April 28.

The wind increasing, furled mizzen topsail at 4 A.M. and at 5 the foresail, both of which were reset at 9. At 11 A.M. set reefed spanker. At 4 P.M. shook reef out of main topsail and foresail. At 5 P.M. furled mainsail and close-reefed main topsail. The wind having increased and the sea running very high, at 8 P.M. furled spanker and mizzen topsail and hove to under forestaysail, close-reefed main topsail and main spencer. The gale was terrible, howling thro' the rigging, the sea one mass of foam and the ship rolling and pitching at a fearful rate. Towards midnight it began to rain and hail. Wind WSW, steering or rather heading from SSE to S by W. To walk decks is next to impossible and to eat in peace still more difficult, for pots and pans, like blessings, take their flight.

Saturday, April 29.

The gale still blowing, remained hove to till 5:30 P.M. when, the wind lulling again, set reefed foresail and, an hour later, reefed spanker and close-reefed mizzen topsails. The day was clear and the Captain was able to get an observation. Sun's Alt. 20°54′, Decl. 14°12′ N. Lat. 54°42′ S. After 5 P.M. we made a SSW course. I never in my life realized before that waves could run so high as they did today, some of which averaged, at the least, 20 feet.

Sunday, April 30.

At 12:30 A.M. shook reef out of foresail and set reefed mainsail. At 4 A.M., beginning to blow hard again, reefed foresail and furled spanker. At 6 A.M. furled mainsail and set close-reefed mizzen topsail. At 9 A.M., the wind lulling, set spanker, mainsail and inner jib, and shook reef out of foresail; called all hands and wore ship, steering NNW. While wearing ship, the forestaysail sheet block struck Gilby in the face, breaking his nose and knocking him insensible. At 10 A.M. shook reef out of main topsail and an hour afterwards took it in again. Toward afternoon the wind increasing, called all hands about 2 o'clock, furled inner jib, mainsail and spanker, and reefed the foresail.

It was no fool of a job to lay aloft, the wind being cold and it raining hard all the time, so when "Grog ho!" was sounded all hands were glad enough to get their dram, at least I was. It still blowing a living gale of wind at 8 P.M., all hands were again called and wore ship, steering SSW. As it was wet and cold and we were shipping seas every minute, grog was again served out, and then the watch went below again. The wind for the last four days has varied from the NW to SW. At 7:30 P.M., the gale increasing, furled mizzen topsail and fore-sail and hove to.

Monday, May 1.

The gale this morning seemed worse than it had ever been before. Squall after squall accompanied by sleet and snow passed over us in rapid succession. At 4 A.M., when I went up to take the lee wheel, it blew so and the ship rocked and pitched so, that the mate told me I might stay under the weather cloth. So I spent my two hours there watching the sea. Several heavy seas struck and washed the whole poop, while forward and amidships all was flooded. Sometimes I could see a huge wave with its white crest coming down upon us and have just time to dodge when it would board us. At daylight it was awful, and we were standing by the main topsail clew lines in case it should be necessary to take it in. Several times we rolled so that we shipped an enormous amount of water to leeward, which poured over the side like a waterfall washing the decks fore and aft. When break-fast was served out our room was in a sad state, chests and all knock-ing about, the floor flooded and every one obliged to hang on like grim Death to his eatables. In spite of all my care a lurch upset Char-ley's cup of coffee into my mush and a wave which we shipped at the time doused me and half filled my pan. The romance of sea life is at an end with me, tho' still I like it, in spite of its evils. This is the fifth day of the gale and the worst one, too. For five long, cold, dreary days with the exception of one or two lulls, have we laid at the mercy of the sea, hove to the greater part of the time. The wind was NW and we were heading S all night. I, for one, shall be most heartily glad when we get clear of the South Pacific. It was a fearful sight to see the huge waves coming down upon us, some of which I am sure must have exceeded 20 feet in height, and then see her roll so that the water would pour over her lee side. Forward was so covered at times with spray that you could hardly see the foremast. Quite a different May Day this is from the one I spent two years ago on the Green at New Haven, and little did I think then that I should be here today. At 4 P.M., the gale beginning to break, set the foresail and at 6 P.M. wore ship, the wind SW by S, and steered our course NNW. A sail was in sight on our lee bow all the afternoon. At 7 P.M. set reefed spanker. At 8 P.M. set close-reefed fore-topsail. Between 8 and 12 P.M. the starboard watch set mainsail, close-reefed mizzen topsail and shook a reef out of foresail and main topsail. Sun's Alt. 19°35'. Decl. 15°7' N. Lat. 55°6' S.

Tuesday, May 2.

At 12 A.M. set inner jib. At 1:30 shook a reef out of mainsail, fore- and mizzen topsails. Between 4 and 8 A.M. shook reef out of fore-, main and mizzen topsails and set all three topgallant sails and outer jib. During the morning rove new topsail clew lines and spencer brails. The day was cloudy and cold, yet all were cheerful because we knew our course W by N was rapidly taking us into warm weather again. The sea has gone down and naught remains to tell of our gale but the long, heavy swell. At 6 P.M., the weather being a little squally, took a single reef in mizzen topsail and furled fore- and mizzen-topgallant sails and outer jib. The mate kept the watch standing by the main-topgallant sail nearly all his four hours, determined to keep it on, and all night long did we plough onwards, 12 knots per hour.

Wednesday, May 3.

Between 12 and 4 A.M. the starboard watch set the fore- and mizzen-topgallant sails, shook the reef out of the mizzen topsail and set main-topmast staysail. At 6 A.M. the crossjack split down the lee leech and was unbent and sent on deck to be mended. At 6:30 the reef was shaken out of spanker and main topsail. At 10 A.M. the crossjack was rebent and set and the remaining reef shaken out of the fore-topsail, so we are at last under whole topsails again. A bark was in sight on our weather beam, homeward bound, under close-reefed topsails. She presented a beautiful sight, pitching up and down. Course NW. The night looking squally, the watch were kept standing by the topgallant halyards nearly all night. At 11:30 P.M. the main-topmast staysail and main spencer were furled.

Thursday, May 4.

The wind began to die away towards morning and we had it only in puffs all the morning. During the afternoon a SE wind sprang up and we steered a NW course. Sun's Alt. 24°59′ (noon). Decl. 16°1′ N. Lat. 48°58′ S. The day was moderately cold and pleasant. The wind freshened towards midnight.

Friday, May 5.

A heavy squall accompanied by rain and hail striking us, at 3 A.M. all hands were called; double-reefed topsails, furled all three top-gallant sails, crossjack, inner and outer jibs. "Grog ho!" as is customary was then sounded and the watch went below. I never felt the cold so much as I did aloft this time. The sleet was blinding and the wind piercing cold and, there being no shelter from it, we were exposed to its full fury. The log was hove at 4 A.M., when we were going 13 knots! At 6 A.M., the wind having moderated tho' still blowing fresh, shook a reef out of main topsail and at 9, one out of fore-topsail and set main-topgallant sail. At 1 P.M., the sea being high and it looking bad to windward, our watch close-reefed fore-topsail. At 4 P.M. reefed main-sail. We were steering from a NNW to a NW by N course all day, with a strong SE wind, going about 12 knots on an average. I spent nearly all the afternoon on topgallant forecastle watching the sea. A heavy swell, fore and aft, kept us pitching, and every wave as it broke was tipped with foam. A myriad of sea birds hovered around, among which I particularly noticed three large albatross with white bodies and black wings, which I am sure must have measured 12 or 18 feet from tip to tip.

Saturday, May 6.

At 1 A.M. set inner jib, shook a reef out of mizzen topsail and set spanker. At 2 A.M. shook another reef out of fore-topsail. At 8 A.M., it being squally, furled main-topgallant sail. At 1 P.M. shook the reef out of mainsail. At 4 P.M. set main-topgallant sail, and a fresh WSW wind, for the wind hauled during the night, sent us flying on our course at the rate of 12 knots per hour. Heavy squalls from the S and W prevailed during the afternoon, accompanied by the heaviest hail I ever saw, and we were steering from a NW by N to a NNW course. The by the N winds which have prevailed for the last day or so. We had for dinner today a strange mixture. As near as I could make it out from the cook, it was meat biscuit dissolved in warm water and mixed with molasses to give it a flavor. About the consistency of mush, it was the vilest compound ever I tasted, and one of which I soon got rid of by throwing it overboard. All I have got to say is, the Lord deliver us, henceforth and forevermore, of such messes. At 12:30 P.M. furled main-topgallant sail. During the night we set all three topgallant sails and the outer jib. The wind was NW and our course N by E. For a little while however we were enabled to steer N and N by W. The way we are fed is truly outrageous. Until the last week the beef has smelt so we could hardly eat it; and tonight, a new barrel of bread being opened, on eating it we found it thickly populated with maggots. Except the first two barrels we have been eating musty bread, which I thought was bad enough, but maggots finish the affair. We are almost as bad off as John was in the ship he came from San Francisco to Panama in. Bad rice, bread and meat are enough to satisfy anyone that Grinnell, Minturn & Co. are a generous firm (over the left.) For the last week or so a regular system of bullying has been tried by a certain individual, which tonight at supper terminated in a fight between him and me, and my mind, for one, is made up that it won't be the last one, either, if he interferes with my affairs any more. "Noli me tangere" is my maxim, and everyone knows the muss was his seeking, not mine. A description of my roommates is needing to make my journal complete, so here goes. George L. Packard is the son of Professor Packard of Bowdoin College and has been several voyages to sea before. He boasts also, in a glorious uncle, no less a personage than Frank Pierce and also another, Abbot Lawrence. He is the personification of Yankee independence and, tho' he has some peculiar eccentricities of his own, nevertheless is an agreeable companion. He is death on a bargain and seldom gives without receiving in return, belying the Scripture that it is more blessed to give than to receive. A second is E. Chichester, a noble, good-hearted fellow, one who never desires to make trouble unless he is meddled with. He was a shipmate of mine in the *Great Republic*, and I was right glad to meet him here. Active enough when he pleases to be, he nevertheless has contracted a habit of putting his hands in his pockets, which has earned him the cognomen of "Hands in Pocket" from a few of us. He is rather short, a little bowlegged, stoops badly and has black hair and eyes, and when rigged out has a decidedly sailorlike look. Next is C. F. Koerner, a German who has made a voyage before in this ship and one in the *Staghound*. He goes by knickname of "Whiskers" because, having a little fuzz, called hair on his chin, he is immoderately proud of it and spends two-thirds of his time brushing it. He is quarrelsome and bullying by disposition and, having tried it with all of us here, has been "bluffed" by all of us. The remaining two are the Glovers, good-hearted fellows from New York, nephews of Purser Barry. Last tho' not least is myself; but I forbear a description.

### Tuesday, May 9.

The sun rose clear today for the first time in a long while. During the morning got up all the royal gear and crossed main royal. During the watch from 12 to 4 P.M. crossed the fore- and mizzen royals, bent the jib topsail and sent up the fore-topmast-studding-sail booms. Wind NW, course N by E. Sun's Alt. 40°40'. Decl. 17°25' N. Lat. 31°43' S. The weather was so warm that I took off all my heavy clothes and put on thin ones. I got my instruments and books again from the boatswain and began studying navigation this afternoon. Starved all day for want of bread, for eat bread with big worms in it I cannot do, and as bread is pretty much our only standby, I had to go without. I wonder what they would say ashore to see their bread, alive. If I had any wish, it was that Grinnell, Minturn & Co. might have nothing else to eat for a week or so.

### Wednesday, May 10.

Towards morning the wind died away and shifted more ahead so we had to steer NNE all the morning, but in the afternoon it came from the W and we were able to steer our course again, NNW. Today has been a busy one. At 4 A.M. set main royals and at 7, fore-royal. During the morning watch from 8 A.M. till noon, our watch sent up fore- and main-topgallant-studding-sail booms, put both quarter boats over the side and bent main-topgallant staysail. The other watch bent all the studding sails except the royal, rove the gear and set mizzen royal, so that a great deal of work has been done for one day. It looked quite like old times to see the royals set, and I am thinking it will be like old times to furl them. Sun's Alt. 42°56'. Decl. 17°41' N. Lat. 29°11' S. The wind being light, we have not averaged over 4 knots all day, rather a falling off from what we have been doing. A perfect God-send! A new cask of fresh bread was opened just before supper, and such a rush as was made to see bread, fresh and clean, I never saw before. Nor am I at all anxious to witness it again.

Thursday, May 11.

A hot, sultry day. The wind died away and we were becalmed nearly all day. In the morning sent down fore- and main-topgallant sails and inner jib, which were new sails, bent for Horn use, and sent up old ones. Got up also the old mainsail and spread it on the poop for repairs preparatory to rebending it. Towards evening light breezes from the NE sprang up and we steered NW. We are expecting the SE trades every day. The starboard watch were kept busy from 8 to 12 (midnight) setting and taking in studding sails, as the wind shifted. Sun's Alt. 44°11'. Decl. 17°56' N. Lat. 27°41' S.

Friday, May 12.

At 1:30 A.M. loosed and set the crossjack and main staysails, which an hour later were furled again. During the morning watch from 8 to 12, rove new mizzen-royal braces, sent the gin down from the main-topsail yard and cleaned it, and then, after shifting the turns out which were in the halyards, reset the sail, got the gig on the poop for the carpenter to repair, rove the old forebraces again and got the mainsail ready to bend. At 1 P.M. set main spencer, sent down the new mainsail and bent the old one. All the afternoon I was busy washing up my dirty clothes, of which I had a great number. A sail was in sight off our lee bow all day. Toward afternoon the wind freshened from NE and we set fore-topmast and -topgallant and main-topgallant studdings, steering a NW course. At 8 P.M. the wind shifted to E by S and we altered our course to NW by W, going at the rate of 10 knots per hour. The trades may now be said to have way and will probably carry us to 10° N. The nearer I get to San Francisco the better I feel, for I long to get my letters and learn all the news at home. Sun's Alt. 44°48'. Decl. 18°17' N. Lat. 26°43' S. At 10 P.M. brailed up main spencer and set main staysails.

1. *Sea Serpent*, pioneer clipper of Grinnell, Minturn & Co.'s California Line and first sharp ship built by George Raynes, Portsmouth, New Hampshire, 1850. Shown passing the South Head, San Francisco, with the Grinnell, Minturn & Co. house flag at her main truck. Pilot schooner is at left. (Oil painting. Mystic Seaport, Mystic, Connecticut)

2. Entry in Gregory's journal for April 9, 1854. (The Mariners Museum)

3. Entry in Gregory's journal for April 9, 1854. (The Mariners Museum)

4. *Sea Serpent* sailing card, November 1864. When competition between various sailing ship lines was at its height, the merchants and owners started to issue colorful cards, about 4″ × 6″, to advertise their vessels. These were distributed among likely shippers and travelers to attract business. (The Mariners Museum)

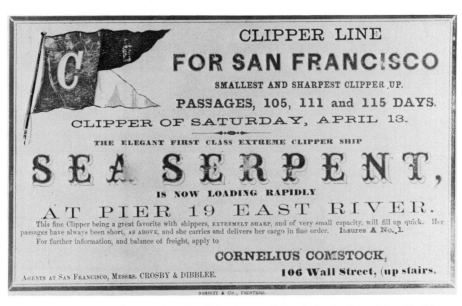

5. *Sea Serpent* sailing card, 1861. (The Seamen's Bank for Savings, New York)

7. *Sea Serpent* sailing card, April 1855. (The Seamen's Bank for Savings, New York)

6. *Sea Serpent* sailing card, 1862. (The Seamen's Bank for Savings, New York)

8. *Corinthian*, built by Blossom, Smith & Dimon, New York, 1822. Built as a packet ship, she became a whaler in 1831 and was wrecked with a large cargo of whale oil in the North Pacific in 1868. The *Sea Serpent* met the *Corinthian* at sea on April 9, 1854. (Oil painting attributed to James F. Pringle, ca. 1829. The Mariners Museum)

# MILLARD FILLMORE,

## PRESIDENT OF THE UNITED STATES OF AMERICA,

### To all who shall see these presents, GREETING

BE IT KNOWN, That leave and permission are hereby given to *Ansel N. Stuart*

master or commander of the *Ship* called *Corinthian*
of the burden of *401 + 32/95*
tons, or thereabouts, lying at present in the port of *New Bedford*
bound for *Pacific Ocean* and laden with

*a intents for a whaling voyage*

to depart and proceed with the said *Ship*
on his said voyage, such *Ship* having been visited,
and the said *Ansel N. Stuart* having made oath before
the proper officer that the said *Ship* belongs
to one or more of the citizens of the United States of America, and to him
or them only.

IN WITNESS WHEREOF, *I have subscribed my name to these presents,
and affixed the seal of the United States of America thereto, and
caused the same to be countersigned by* Mr. *T. Russell Co.*
at *New Bedford* the *3d* day of
*June* *in the year of our Lord* *1851*.

*Millard Fillmore*

9. Sea letter issued to the whale ship *Corinthian* in 1851. This multilingual document in four parallel columns bore the same message in French, Spanish, English, and Dutch, and was signed by the president, secretary of state, and collector of customs. The document permitted the master of the ship, Captain Stuart, to transact business in foreign ports. (The Mariners Museum)

10. The Golden Gate, entrance to the Bay of San Francisco, 1855. View is looking toward the bay from off Point Lobos, with the steamer *John L. Stephens* and the clipper ship *Flying Cloud* just entering the strait. Pilot boat is in left foreground. (Lithograph, after drawing by Thomas A. Ayres. The Mariners Museum)

11. *John L. Stephens*, wooden sidewheel steamer of the Pacific Mail Steamship Company, built by Smith & Dimon, New York, 1852. Gregory saw this steamer in San Francisco on July 1, 1854. (Line engraving. The Mariners Museum)

12. Broadway wharf, San Francisco, at which the *Sea Serpent* lay from June 21 to July 3, 1854, is to the right, with the covered shed at its end. This photograph was taken from Telegraph Hill in 1863. (California Historical Society, San Francisco)

Saturday, May 13.

The wind heading us off more to the N, we were obliged to alter our course to NW by W and take in all the studding sails. Our watch had to slush down in the afternoon, and as usual I had to shoulder a bucket and go aloft. If there is anything I hate to do, it is to slush down, for it is the dirtiest job we have and one most destructive to clothes. In the afternoon the wind came in squalls and we clewed up the royals. Sun's Alt. 46°53'. Decl. 18°26' N. Lat. 24°29' S. Thermometer 74°. Average speed 8 knots. About sundown a large English bark passed us, evidently a guano vessel, homeward bound, but tho' quite near we were unable to make out her name. I began my letter writing today so as to have a batch ready for mailing when we reach San Francisco, and, as I wrote, many a familiar face rose to my memory, of those to whom I was writing. The weather this side is different from what it was the other, for here, tho' it is very hot, it is almost always cloudy, the sun very seldom shining from a cloudless sky, which was the case two-thirds of the time in the Atlantic.

Sunday, May 14.

A lovely day. All hands seemed to be possessed of a cleaning mania. The ship was covered with beds, blankets and clothes spread out to air, while every bucket was in use and all hands washing and shaving. Dick Lyman opened a barber shop in the boatswain's locker and one after another of the forward hands came out, with his hair cut, à la Phalon. Light breezes from the E sent us on our way at the rate of 4 knots. Sun's Alt. 48°40'. Decl. 18°41' N. Lat. 22°27' S. In the evening sent up starboard studding sails. The trades seem to be very light so far, hardly enough to be even called steady winds. Somehow or other I always enjoy Sunday, for as there is no work doing I have a chance to read or write without being disturbed. Long. 86°42' W. We have yet about 24 degrees of longitude to make before we cross the Line. Towards night set starboard studding sails again.

Monday, May 15.

Early in the morning watch unbent the foresail and fore-topsail and sent up old sails. In the afternoon we were busy setting up the mizzen rigging. This time I got clear of the work, for I was forward helping

Frank seize the mats on the foresail, which we managed to make an
8-bell job. The weather was sultry. Sun's Alt. 49°28′. Decl. 18°55′ N.
Lat. 21°25′ S. Towards evening the wind died away and we were entirely becalmed. During the evening, like a prudent person, I rolled up
my sleeves and went into the washing business and did nothing but
scrub, scrub for over two hours, when I had the satisfaction of hanging up to dry a dozen articles of clothing, all the stock I had on hand.
The washing business is a great one. At 11 P.M. took in all the studding
sails.

Tuesday, May 16.

We were busy all the morning making sennit, foxes, mending old
studding sails, and, having sent down the mizzen-topgallant sail early
in the first watch, all those who could use a palm were occupied in
altering it so as to make it fit better. The water was a smooth as glass
and hardly a ripple disturbed its surface; in fact, I never saw the sea
so smooth since we sailed from New York. At the present rate we will
see San Francisco somewhere near doomsday. The Captain says these
are the queerest trades he ever saw, neither blowing one way or another. Certain it is they do not stand as friendly to us as we expected.
While I am writing I can hear Mr. Cornell's canary singing away as if
it would split its throat, and it reminds me of home, where our little
birds used to chirp so cheerfully.

Wednesday, May 17.

At noon we began to set up rigging. Between 12 and 4 P.M. we set
up the starboard lower main rigging, which, I think, was quick work
considering the smallness of the watch. The whole day was calm, with
occasionally a cat's-paw which would fill our sails for a few minutes
and then pass away. Sun's Alt. 50°1′. Decl. 19°24′ N. Lat. 20°23′ S.
Thermometer 76°. Setting up rigging is a laborious as well as a dirty
occupation, for you have to heave at the capstan two-thirds of the time,
and one's hands suffer, for the tar burns into the skin and nails, color-
ing them a dingy yellow. It is really too provoking to be merely floating like a log with the current, making but little headway; it's worse

than a gale, for then there is something to excite one. The cook killed two pigs for a fresh mess tomorrow, and more than one began to say we would have a breeze, which sure enough was the case, for towards midnight a breeze sprang up from E by S.

### Thursday, May 18.

At 12:30 A.M. hoisted starboard studding sails and once more our good ship went her way, to the great joy of all hands, for we had made up our minds to at least four days more calm, when the moon would change. Between 8 and 12 our watch set up port main rigging. At 9 A.M. a ship hove in sight off our weather bow and by 11 A.M. passed us about 4 miles distant. He was a whaler by all appearances, for he only had short sail, being under a main-topgallant sail. The Captain said he never knew a pig to be killed but a spouter hove in sight before it was eat up, which has proved the case twice with us. Sun's Alt. 51°9′. Decl. 19°37′ N. Lat. 19°2′ S. Wind E by S. Course NW ½ N. The starboard watch were busy setting up mizzen-topmast rigging all the afternoon. When our watch came on deck at 4 P.M. the mate gave orders to get up the main-royal-studding-sail gear and send up the booms. By 5 o'clock all was ready and we set the starboard studding sail, being the first time one has been up this voyage and the first time the Captain has sailed under one, at least so he says. We have now good hopes of crossing the Line in about nine days more, for we average 9 knots per hour and the wind continues to be steady.

### Friday, May 19.

A cloudy day. In the afternoon put up the main-topmast-studding-sail booms and then set lee main-royal, -topgallant and -topmast and weather -topmast studding sails, so that now we seem to be one huge cloud of canvas. Today numbers of boobies and Mother Carey's chickens made their appearance. Wind SE by E. Course NW by N. Speed 9½ to 10 knots. Sun's Alt. 53°39′. Decl. 19°49′ N. Lat. 16°20′ S. Thermometer 74°. It is fun to be hastening onward at the rate we are now with so much canvas as we spread. Towards night clewed up all the after sails so as to allow full chance for the sails on the mainmast to draw. During the night it was rainy.

Saturday, May 20.

Today commenced tarring down, Bob and Charley tarring the miz-zen-royal and -topgallant backstays, lifts and footropes. Bob upset his bucket over the deck, spars, sails, etc., for which he got a hearty blessing from the Captain, mate and, last but not least, us boys, for we had to clean up the poop after him, which was an 8-bell job. It was lucky he was on board the *Sea Serpent* or he would have had to clean it up in his watch below. I went into the cabin to get some white pants out but, when I got them, found they were of no use, being a size too large. Wind SE by E. Course NW. Speed about 8 knots.

Sunday, May 21.

A lovely day. Sun's Alt. 58°32'. Decl. 20°14' N. Lat. 11°2' S. Wind and course the same. I busied myself nearly all day writing letters home and overhauling my chest. The weather was very warm and uncomfortable.

Monday, May 22.

Sun's Alt. 60°35'. Decl. 20°26' N. Lat. 8°47' S. Wind and course the same. In the morning our watch were busy turning in the main-topmast backstays and rattling down main rigging, which latter work was continued by the other watch. I think I never suffered so with heat as I did today. About 11 o'clock unbent main-topmast staysail and bent an old one in its place, which by the way the men who bent it, bent with its head down. The mate when he saw it was outrageously mad and gave it to them hot and heavy, telling them he thought A.S. (able seaman) in their case meant what it spelt. Several times during the day the main staysails and jibs were lowered and reset, according, as the wind hauled ahead a little or not. We are now rapidly approaching the Line and all hands are busy calculating the number of days which must elapse ere we pass the Golden Gate and see the El Dorado of America.

Tuesday, May 23.

A hot sultry day. Bonitos having been seen around the ship, I took my line and was lucky enough to catch three large ones and unlucky enough to lose two larger ones and all my hooks. There was considerable excitement in catching them, for they were about a foot and a half long and pulled very hard. They were in pursuit of flying fish, which I saw for the first time in the Pacific. All day long both watches were busy tarring down mizzen rigging, which with the exception of the lanyards was finished, and turning in main backstays. Knapp and myself were busy serving anew the fore-topmast stay, and it was no fool of a job, hanging in the air on almost nothing for the four hottest hours of the day, viz: from noon till 4 P.M., exposed to the full heat of the sun. For supper we had fried bonito and to me it was a most agreeable change. The whole crew had a mess of them. Sun's Alt. 62°35'. Decl. 20°38' N. Lat. 6°35' S. Wind and course the same.

### Wednesday, May 24.

Busy tarring down main rigging and backstays. I was put to finish the mizzen lanyards and tho' a dirty job nevertheless it became an agreeable one, for the Captain came and talked to me nearly all the time. He told me to tell Father that he thought I would sooner patronize an oyster shop than a hospital. He told me, too, many a story about his son, Bob, to whom he seems to be much attached. The men were at work all the morning turning in main and fore backstays. Saw a couple of man-of-war hawks hovering over the ship towards sunset. Lat. 4° 30' S. Wind hauling to the E during the night.

### Thursday, May 25.

Tarring down again all day. Tarred down mainstays and mizzen stays in the morning and forestays and jibstays in the afternoon. Between noon and 4 P.M. set up starboard fore rigging and began painting the gig. Sun's Alt. 67°1'. Decl. 21° N. Lat. 1°47' S. Thermometer 85°. Wind SE. Course NW. Towards noon saw tremendous schools of flying fish rise in every direction, indeed I never saw so many before in my life. Bonitos were obviously the cause of their alarm. In the afternoon I saw a double rainbow in the E, the first one I have seen in the Pacific. Long. 100°37' W. The trades begin to grow lighter and for the last twenty-four hours we have averaged about 5½ knots per hour. Wind hauling to the S towards night. The wind being aft, have made but little use of our staysails and jibs but have piled studding sails upon her, having set this afternoon three more port fore studding sails, which makes eleven altogether.

Friday, May 26.

Crossed the Line at 10:30 A.M., in Long. 101°15′ W. This makes the second time for me, and twice more must I cross it ere I see home again. Our watch were at work all the morning setting up port fore rigging and topmast backstays. It was awful hot work heaving on the capstan exposed to the full power of the sun's rays. A most amusing incident occurred while we were at work; Major made his appearance dressed up in coat, pants, and hat, which some mischievous sailor had put on him, and walked up and down, as grave as a parson, to the great amusement of all hands. Weather hot, with frequent squalls of rain. Wind from S. Course NW. Lat. 5° N. At 6 P.M. took in lee fore studding sails. The trades have left us and we are on what Maury calls debatable ground. However, we appear to be in luck's way and "luck is everything."

Saturday, May 27.

A sultry day. Sun's Alt. 71°41′. Decl. 21°2′ N. Lat. 3°14′ N. Wind S. Course NW. Speed 9 knots. At 8 A.M. took in all lee studding sails, braced yards and set main staysails and jibs. Tarred down fore-royal, topgallant and -topsail lifts and footropes and -topmast rigging and backstays. We are nearly done our tarring down (thank Providence) and may expect to keep clean the rest of the voyage. At the present rate, the Captain thinks seventeen more will see us in California.

Sunday, May 28.

This morning about 4 A.M. the 3d mate and some of his watch had a fight, which caused great excitement, all hands being on deck looking on. The 2d mate came forward and put a stop to it, tho' not without hot words on both sides. At noon a heavy rainsquall passed over us and, the wind hauling ahead, took in all the studding sails and main staysails. It poured a perfect deluge and was such a warm rain that I stripped to my pants and went under the spout and washed myself and all my dirty clothes. The watch on deck filled all the empty water casks. It rained hard all night and, tho' wet thro', still I went to sleep on a pile of boards, a most imprudent thing.

Monday, May 29.

Still raining. At 8 A.M. furled royals, jib topsail, staysails, and sent down royal-studding-sail booms. The horizon was one mass of black clouds, the wind light and shifting from one point to the other between S and W. Astern of us, too far off to distinguish clearly, was a large waterspout, the first one I ever saw. A large bark passed to leeward of us, distant about 7 miles, standing SSW about noon. At noon it cleared off and was very hot. Sun's Alt. 76°3'. Decl. 21°39' N. Lat. 7°54' N. Wind during the afternoon SW by W. Course NW by N. Average speed 6 knots. At 3 P.M. set royals and jib topsail again. The rain gave all hands a chance to wash clothes, and from early in the morning to late at night the ship seemed one huge washtub. The royal studding sails were sent down and stowed away, and everything is being got in readiness for the NE trades, which we expect daily, as we are in the proper track of them. The wind towards the middle of the afternoon died away and we had rain again.

Tuesday, May 30.

At 5 A.M. a light breeze sprang up from the same quarter as before and it cleared off. All the forenoon and afternoon watches were busy making new spanker vangs, sending down main-topmast-studding-sail booms and gear, and spreading all the studding sails out to dry. Also, rove new fore-topsail halyards and set main staysails. Sun's Alt. 77°20'. Decl. 21°48' N. Lat. 9°20' N. Course NW by N. Speed about 3 knots. Billy Clohecy laid down on a knife that was laying in his bunk and cut himself severely, so much so that for the rest of the voyage he will have to lay up.

Wednesday, May 31.

Today the wind was baffling, first on one quarter then on the other, and two-thirds of the time we did not average over 1½ knots. It was so extremely hot that but little work was done, except tarring and setting up the fore-royal and fore-topgallant stays. The boatswain got in a rage at the boys several times to our great amusement, as he made a complete fool of himself. At 10 P.M. furled royals, crossjack and main staysails. One of the sailors showed me the North Star and the Great Dipper. They have been in sight for a long time, the latter having been seen in about 12° S. I almost imagined I was home again, it seemed so familiar, the very name of the Dipper. I begin to fear that we are going to have a long calm, from all indications. Sun's Alt. 78°40′. Decl. 21°57′ N. Lat. 10°49′ N.

Thursday, June 1.

That first day of summer. Flora is holding her revels at home and has covered the earth with her varied offerings which I used to love so well to gather. I would love dearly to have one more ramble in the woods, but here I am at sea. The wind was very light from the N until noon, when, joy of joys, the long-wished-for trades struck us and soon we were dancing merrily on our way. At 12:30 P.M. the royals were loosed and sheeted home. All hands felt joyful; the doldrums were at an end and we were once more flying for San Francisco. Sun's Alt. 78°50′. Decl. 22°6′ N. Lat. 11°8′ N. Long. 110°8′15″ W.

Friday, June 2.

At 7:30 A.M. set main spencer. A man-of-war hawk was hovering over us for some time and then flew away. This makes the third day that one has done so, a curious circumstance. Sun's Alt. 80°10′. Decl. 22°14′ N. Lat. 12°36′ N. At 9 P.M. brailed up main spencer. Long. 112°18′30″ W. Wind N and E, steering full and by.

Saturday, June 3.

At 2 A.M. set crossjack. Sun's Alt. 81°27′. Decl. 22°21′ N. Lat. 14° N. Wind N by E. Course NW. Average speed 8 knots. Busy all day tarring down, which we finished, and painting the masts. Today, as a very great treat, we had mackerel for dinner. A booby alighting on the mizzen-royal yardarm, Jack Glover went up and caught him. Long. 114°45′ W.

Sunday, June 4.

While washing decks, about a hundred porpoises in one huge school passed us. It was a pretty sight to see them jumping and rolling about in the water. At 9 A.M. an accident happened to me which I shall not forget for a long while. I was forward, sitting on one of the head guys, talking to Bill Clohecy, the ship going about 10 knots and a heavy swell from the N at the time, when a wave struck us and carried me off with it. I sunk a tremendous distance and rose about ten feet astern of the ship. The 2d mate threw a brace to me, but I missed it; and when I rose on the next wave, the *Sea Serpent* was at least five or six times her length from me, and I could see a boat lowering and that she was hove to. Stripping myself, I struck out for a bench which the 3d mate had thrown overboard and, after two or three minutes hard work, reached it and then felt myself safe! In about five minutes I was in the boat and soon reached the ship, which went on her course again. For the first second or so, after I missed the brace, I thought my chances were poor; but when I saw the boat lowering, I knew I was safe, for I felt I could swim well nigh an hour before I would sink and in less than that time, in all probability, I should be picked up. The Captain was very anxious, so the boys told me, being as pale as a sheet and hardly able to speak. Indeed, it was only a miracle that I was saved, for had it been blowing hard or been squally it would have been impossible to have lowered a boat and my chances for life would have been indeed slight. However, a "miss is as good as a mile" and here I am, safe and sound, thankful for my escape. Soon after I got on board the Captain came forward with a bundle of Testaments and Tracts which he distributed among the crew. When I first sank, thoughts of home, of sharks and of what my fate was to be, darted over my mind, but when I arose and found myself clear of the ship, of course every thought was directed to save myself. I did not think the boat would be lowered till they had got the ship hove to, we were going so fast, and I directed every energy to a long struggle, expecting to be a long while in the water, the ship being so far ahead and going a knot or so, even when hove to, and the swell carrying me from her rapidly. Everything happened providentially for me, it being extremely lucky that someone saw me fall. Billy says he was laughing at the idea of my getting a ducking, never for an instant dreaming I was overboard till Manuel thoughtfully looked over the side for me and gave the alarm. To him I probably owe my life, in a great degree. Lat. 15°39′ N. Course NW by N. Long. 115°40′ W.

Monday, June 5.

Early this morning unbent main spencer and then began to scrub paintwork, which is a tiresome, dirty job. However, I was too thankful that I was even on board to growl at any labor, no matter how disagreeable it was. Wind from N and E. Course varying from WNW to NW by N. Average speed 7 knots. Lat. 17° N. Long. 117°5′ W. They are beginning to light up on our food, for yesterday we had plum duff, today macaroni soup, for dinner. At 6 P.M. furled crossjack.

Tuesday, June 6.

The wind was very strong from the N accompanied by a heavy swell from N and E. At 7:30 A.M. furled fore- and mizzen royals and at 8, the main royal. It took four of us to furl the fore as it had ripped and got foul of the yard, and it was no fool of a job we had, the ship was pitching so. At 12:30 P.M. the weather earing of the fore-topsail parted, together with the rovings, as far as the middle of yardarm. Laid aloft and, after a couple of hours hard work, succeeded in passing a new earing and double-reefing the sail. At 3 P.M. furled fore- and mizzen-topgallant sails. The inner jib split in the latter part of the forenoon watch, and the watch on deck unbent it and bent a new one. Finished scrubbing paintwork and unrove all the weather studding-sail gear during the afternoon. Sun's Alt. 85°58′. Decl. 22°41′ N. Lat. 18°51′ N. Long. 119°40′ W. Wind N. Course NW and NW by W. Average speed 8 knots.

Wednesday, June 7.

At 6 A.M. shook reefs out of fore-topsail. The wind blew a fresh gale from the N and we were shipping water all the time, so much so that all hands knocked off work and went under shelter. At 12:30 P.M. a crash was heard and, on looking to see what was the matter, found the fore-topsail had split from head to foot, in the middle, and was fast going to pieces. All hands were called and after two hours work got what was left of it on deck, got up a new one and bent it, single-reefed. No sooner had we got thro' than "The main-topgallant sail is ripping" was sung out and we had to clew it up and two or three hands laid aloft to repair it, after which it was furled. Hurra! for Frisco! Here we are going nearly 2 degrees of latitude and longitude every day, close-hauled at that. The weather is so cold that I have been obliged to put on woolen clothes to keep warm. Lat. 21° N. Speed 9 knots.

Thursday, June 8.

At 7 A.M. set main-topgallant sail. At 11 A.M. set fore- and mizzen-topgallant sails. Sun's Alt. 43°40'. Decl. 22°52' N. Lat. 23°16' N. Long. 124°19'45" W. San Francisco bearing at noon N ½ E. Dist. 880 miles. Course NW ½ W. Wind N ½ E. Speed 9 knots. In the afternoon watch sent down fore- and main-topgallant-studding-sail booms and scraped and greased them.

Friday, June 9.

Busy all day cleaning ship, scraping the royal, topgallant and top-masts, (main- and mizzen-), the wheel and the after capstan. During the morning sent down the fore-royal, which was examined and condemned as unfit for use. We are now rapidly nearing our haven, and a week from today hope to see land once more. Wind N. Course NW by W. Speed 8 knots. Lat. 25°6' N. Long. 127° W.

Saturday, June 10.

Cleaning ship all day long. In the afternoon finished scraping the masts and jibboom and greased them; also bent a new fore-royal. The boatswain and I were at work the greater part of the afternoon on the mizzen-royal getting the bolt out of the masthead so as to rig a new sheave for the halyards. First thing I knew a block which he had carried up to rig temporary halyards in came whizzing by my head and, striking the rim of the top, struck the quarter boat and bounced overboard. Had it fallen on deck, nine chances out of ten it would have struck one of the men who were mending the jib. A careless affair, I think, and a thing which, if a boy had done it, he would never have heard the last of. The wind is gradually failing and hauling ahead making our course about NW by W ½ W. Average speed 6 knots. Lat. 26°47' N. Long. 129°39'15" W (9 A.M.).

Sunday, June 11.

A cloudy day. The wind very light from N. At 9 A.M. loosed and set royals. At 6 P.M., the wind heading us off, tacked ship, standing to the NE. At 11:45 P.M. tacked ship again and steered NW. Sun's Alt. 84°57′. Decl. 23°7′ N. Lat. 27°58′ N. Long. 131° W. The wind very light and baffling. San Francisco bearing NE ¾ N. Dist. 718 miles.

Monday, June 12.

Almost becalmed, there being hardly wind enough to fill the sails. Saw numbers of gooneys, a black bird about as large as a duck, flying around the ship. Lat. 28°36′. About 9 P.M. the wind sprang up again from the N and E and by midnight was so strong that the royals were furled.

Tuesday, June 13.

A beautiful day. A strong wind sent us flying on a NW by N course at the rate of 8 knots per hour. Both watches busy all day cleaning ship, painting, varnishing gratings and overhauling the windlass; a dirty job! At 7 A.M. set the royals. Lat. 30°54′ N. Long. 134°24′ W.

Wednesday, June 14.

Light breezes. In the afternoon got the starboard anchor shipped ready for the chains; also scrubbed and painted the quarter boats. Lat. 32°51′ N.

Thursday, June 15.

Light breezes and at times totally becalmed. Oh! how provoking it is, almost in sight of port, so to say, and yet unable to move. At 9 A.M. called all hands and went about on larboard tack, standing to N and E. At 1 P.M. went about again on starboard tack, steering a NW course. At 11:45 P.M. squared the after yards, the wind having all died away. Lat. 33°43′ N.

Friday, June 16.

At 2 A.M. braced around on larboard tack, a light breeze having sprung up from the N and W, which allowed us to steer a NE by N course. Both watches busy thro' the day, scraping jibboom, belaying pins, making harbor gaskets and painting. Lat. 33°50′ N. The wind was baffling all the afternoon and we were braced first one way and then another till 6 P.M., when a NNW breeze sprang up and we went about again on larboard tack, steering NE by N.

## Saturday, June 17.

Early this morning, about 4 A.M., set the crossjack. At 10 A.M. discovered a sail on our weather bow, steering the same course as ourselves. As the Captain remarked, here is a chance for a race. We were gaining slowly on her, for when first seen only a speck could be discovered on the horizon and at noon you could make out her hull and spars from the deck. Busy all day, painting, scraping belaying pins, stowing water casks, so as to get decks clear, getting out mooring chains and hawsers and stowing the sails anew in the after hatch. Lat. 35°8′ N. Long. 135°53′ W. Wind NNW. Course NE by N. Average speed 5 knots. San Francisco distance 668.2 miles. Course E 75°56′ N or nearly E by N ¼ N. During the first dogwatch sent up fore- and main-topgallant-studding-sail booms (weather) and rove the gear. At 7 P.M. passed the sail which we saw in the morning; she proved to be a Belgian bark; showed our ensign and burgee, or private signal. She showed some private signals which, of course, we forward knew nothing about.

## Sunday, June 18.

At 3 A.M. set fore-topgallant studding sail. When our watch turned out at daylight, our friend the Belgian was out of sight. Wind WNW. Average speed 8 knots. Course NE by E. San Francisco bearing E by N ¾ N. Dist. 480 miles. Lat. 36°44′ N. Long. 132°22′ W. The weather was hazy all day and very damp.

## Monday, June 19.

At 4:30 A.M. the starboard watch began to get up the chain cables. When our watch came on deck at 8 o'clock they had enough out of the locker for us to take a turn around the windlass and shackle onto the anchors. Which having done, we laid aft to the capstan and were busy till noon getting the cables on deck. Got out 60 fathoms of the starboard and 75 of the larboard chain. While heaving on the capstan the boatswain gave orders for only one man to stay at a bar, the rest to go forward and help stow the chain on deck. For some reason or other, best known to himself, Charley Koerner did not go. I said to him (in fun), "Lay forward, Charley," to which he replied, "I'll see you d——d, first," or something to that effect. About ten minutes after, the boatswain came aft in a tearing rage saying, "Mr. K., lay forward, I'll teach you better than to send me a message, 'to be d——d.' " Charley told him that he never said anything about him, whereupon the boatswain kicked him. Charley then went forward. He has drawn up a statement of the facts, which has been signed by all who saw it, and intends to put the case in Manchester's hands, the sailor's lawyer, and make the boatswain pay for it. It was a most outrageous affair and one which the Captain should give his attention to, and see justice done to Charley Koerner.

### Ben Bolt

Don't you remember sweet Alice, Ben Bolt?
　Sweet Alice, with hair so brown.
Who blushed with delight if you gave her a smile,
　And trembled with fear at your frown?
In the old churchyard in the valley, Ben Bolt,
　In a corner obscure and lone,
They have fitted a slab of granite so gray,
　And Alice lies under the stone.

Under the hickory tree, Ben Bolt,
　That stood at the foot of the hill.
Together we've lain in the noonday shade,
　And listened to Appleton's mill.
The mill wheel has fallen to pieces, Ben Bolt,
　The rafters have tumbled in
And a quiet that crawls round the wall as you gaze,
　Takes the place of the olden din.

Do you mind the cabin of logs, Ben Bolt,
　That stood in the pathless wood?
And the buttonball tree with its motley boughs
　That night by the doorstep stood?
That cabin to ruin has gone, Ben Bolt,
　You would look for the tree in vain;

> And where once the lords of the forest stood,
>   Grows grass and the golden grain.
>
> And don't you remember the school, Ben Bolt,
>   And the master, so cruel and grim?
> And the shady nook in the running brook,
>   Where the children went to swim?
> Grass grows on the masters grave, Ben Bolt.
>   The spring of the brook is dry;
> And of all the boys who were schoolmates then,
>   There are only you and I!
>
> There's a change in the things I love, Ben Bolt!
>   They have changed from the old to the new;
> But I feel in the core of my spirit the truth,
>   There never was a change in you.
> Twelve months, twenty have passed, Ben Bolt,
>   Since first we were friends, yet I hail
> Thy presence a blessing, thy friendship a truth,
>   Ben Bolt of the salt sea gale!

Wind WNW. Course NE by E. Average speed 9 knots. Lat. 37°33′ N. Long. 129°10′ W. Distance run 176 miles.

Tuesday, June 20.

During the morning watch set the fore-topmast studding. At 9 A.M. set main-topgallant studding sail. During the afternoon watch, set fore lower studding sail and sent up lee fore-and main-topgallant booms. Lat. 37°47′ N. Wind NW. Course ENE. Weather misty and foggy.

Wednesday, June 21.

Glory of glories! At 9 A.M. passed the Farallon Islands and half an hour after took a pilot on board. At 1 P.M. began to shorten sail and at 2 were alongside Broadway wharf. No sooner were we fast, than Mr. Vincent made his appearance with letters from home. They were dated May 2d and all were well. Went ashore in the evening and saw the city. The principal places of resort I found to be the gambling houses and, under the guidance of one who had been in the city before, I started to see those of most repute, viz: the Eldorado, Arcade, Polka, etc. The rooms were crowded, and money seemed to fly so to speak. Heavy bets were won and lost in a turn of a card, and money changed hands to a great amount.

Thursday, June 22.

Began discharging cargo. Went up to the post office and got a letter from Captain Glynn enclosing two letters of introduction. Called on Mr. Vincent, not in. In the evening went on board the *Coeur de Lion* to see Mr. Crawford, her 2d mate, whom I became acquainted with at Corner's in Boston.

Friday, June 23.

Discharging cargo. Got liberty all day. In the morning called on Mr. Vincent, who introduced me to Mr. Hale, his partner, a most pleasant man. Also called on Mrs. Hooper, who received me very kindly. In the afternoon presented my letter of introduction to Flint, Peabody & Co., seeing first Mr. Kellog, who was very polite and introduced me to Mr. Flint. I enquired at the post office for Ed. Eld and found that he did not live in the city but in one of the neighboring villages or ranches and sent up by express for his letters every once in a while.

Saturday, June 24.

Discharging cargo.

Sunday, June 25.

Spent at Mrs. Hooper's. Went to church twice; in the morning heard Bishop Kip, in the evening Rev. Mr. Moore.

Monday, June 26.

Discharging cargo.

Tuesday, June 27.

Commenced to take in ballast. The stevedores finished discharging cargo tonight.

Wednesday, June 28.

Taking in ballast. The mate gave me a good job to take an account of how many tons are taken in, a very agreeable job as all I have to do is to sit still from one day's beginning to its end and give each driver a ticket when he drops his load.

Thursday, June 29.

Taking in ballast and quicksilver.

Friday, June 30.

Finished taking in ballast, 375 tons in all.

Saturday, July 1.

Early this morning the Pacific Mail Line ship *John L. Stephens* arrived with the mails from home. Went ashore in the afternoon and bid all my friends good-bye.

Sunday, July 2.

Never felt so discouraged in my life. I was so confident that I should get letters that a refusal never entered my head, when all my hopes were dashed by a cool, "None for you." If those at home only knew how I had set my heart on a letter by the mail and how bitterly I was disappointed, they would not have forgotten me so soon.

Monday, July 3.

At 6 A.M. the steamer *Hercules* took us in tow and proceeded down the harbor. At 1 o'clock to my great pleasure we cast loose from the steamer and were once more at sea under full sail. At 2, the wind increasing, furled royals; at 3 P.M., the mizzen- and fore-topgallant sails. At 4 P.M., the wind blowing a gale, the main-topgallant sail split in two. At 5 P.M. called all hands and double-reefed topsails and furled outer jibs. I was so sick that after reefing topsails I turned in. We have three cabin passengers, Messrs. Hooper, Howard and Allen, and sixty Chinese in the steerage. At 8 P.M. the mizzen topsail split and was furled. Wind NE. Course SW by S.

Tuesday, July 4.

A very different Fourth from any I ever spent before. The wind was very strong and the sea heavy till late in the afternoon, at 4 P.M., when we set whole topsails and topgallant sails. During the forenoon watch sent down the mizzen topsail and bent a new one. At 2 P.M. sent down main-topgallant sail and bent a new one. I was so much under the weather by afternoon that I turned in again and was sick all night with dysentery accompanied by cramps. With all this, too, I had a twinge of homesickness; I could not but feel bad at the idea that I had received no letters from home. Wind NE. Course SW by S. Speed 10 knots per hour. Lat. 35°25′ N.

Wednesday, July 5.

Sick all day. The Captain gave me a dose of calomel, which kept me from going on deck all day. During the afternoon squared the yards and set fore lower, -topmast and -topgallant studding sails (starboard). During the night the lower studding sail ripped and was taken down. Wind, course and average speed the same as yesterday. Lat. 32°55′ N.

Thursday, July 6.

In the morning the watch were busy repairing the sails that had ripped. At 4 P.M. set weather and lee main-topgallant studding sails. At 6 P.M. clewed up mizzen topsail and furled mizzen royal and -top-gallant sail and furled fore-royal and clewed up -topgallant sail; also took in all the fore studding sails; as the wind is dead aft none of these sails is of material use. Came off the sick list in the morning. Winds, course and speed about the same as usual. Got both anchors on the bows and stowed the cables in the locker.

Friday, July 7.

In the watch from 12 to 4 P.M. the main-topmast-studding-sail booms were sent up, and at 6 P.M. sent up the studding sails. At 7 P.M. furled fore-topgallant sail. All night long we, poor creatures in our room, had a concert, for, the hen coop being front of our quarters, we of course had a full share of rooster, hen, goose, and duck melody; added to all this the Chinese brought a grizzly bear (a cub) which one of them owned and sat his cage by the hen coop, and such a outrageous racket as he raised was a caution, and Fanny, Mr. Hooper's terrier, of course joined concert. There was verily no peace for the wicked. First one and then another would get up and poke the confounded bear, and at last one genius suggested that "he guessed he'd stop if he was ducked," a suggestion the sense of which all saw and which was immediately tried with entire success. Wind and course continued the same. Average speed 9 knots.

### Saturday, July 8.

Set fore (weather and lee) lower and (weather) -topmast studding sails and hauled up the mainsail at 2 P.M. At 10 P.M. boarded main tacks, loosed and set the mizzen royal and -topgallant sail, the wind having hauled a little on the starboard quarter. Wind NE. Course SW ½ W. Speed 10 knots.

### Sunday, July 9.

At 5 A.M. clewed up the after sails and hauled up the mainsail. At 7 A.M. the port fore lower studding sail ripped all to pieces; took it in, bent and set a new one at 8 A.M. In the first dogwatch, from 4 P.M. to 6, sent up main-royal-studding-sail booms and, after reeving the gear, set the sails both sides.

### Monday, July 10.

A beautiful, sunny day. At 10 A.M. loosed and set fore-topgallant sail and mizzen royal and -topgallant sail. Also unbent the crossjack. I never saw such a filthy, loathsome set of creatures as the Chinamen we have on board are. And such a chattering as they keep up night and day is enough to make one cut his throat in despair. Lat. 20°57′ N. Wind NE. Course SW ½ W. Average speed 7 knots.

### Tuesday, July 11.

At 10 A.M. set port fore-topmast studding sail. At 1 P.M. clewed up after sails and furled the royal and topgallant sail. Towards night the Captain began to shorten sail, furling royals and taking in all the studding sails. We are now within a few hours sail of the Sandwich

Islands, and as a rumor has been going the rounds that we were to heave to off Honolulu and send a boat ashore, all hands were getting letters ready for home. Not so with me; for several reasons I did not write. Wind E. Course SW ½ W. Average speed 9 knots.

Wednesday, July 12.

At 4 A.M. set main royal. At 9 A.M. land was in plain sight both sides of us, and we were rapidly passing between two large islands, the names of which no one seemed to know. I could see green fields, and high above the clouds that lingered around its base the top of a lofty mountain showed itself. The wind was so strong and favorable that the Captain gave up all idea of stopping, much to the disappointment of our letter writers. By night all that was visible was the top of the mountain. We then began to set sail and by midnight had all the studding sails set again. Wind N and E. Course SW by W.

Thursday, July 13.

At 9 A.M. set mizzen royal and -topgallant sail and fore-royal. The wind hauled to the N more during the night and we altered our course to WSW. During the first dogwatch, we bent the crossjack again. Lat. 18°33′ N. At 7 P.M. clewed up after sails.

Friday, July 14.

Very warm. Busy making sennit all day. At 9 A.M. clewed up fore-royal and -topgallant sail. Wind N and E. Course W by S ½ S. Average speed 8 knots per hour.

Saturday, July 15.

A hot day. Cleaned the ship's tools and made sennit. Wind ENE. Course W by S ½ S. Average speed 7 knots.

Sunday, July 16.

A beautiful day. An 8-knot breeze sent us spinning on our course, (W by S ½ S). I read over my letters from home again, and, strange to say, tho' I know them almost by heart, still they were interesting as ever. Long. 166°29′ W.

### Monday, July 17.

Long. 169°23′ W. Lat. 17°56′ N.

### Tuesday, July 18.

Long. 172°11′ W. Course W by S ½ S. Average speed 7 knots. Took my first weather wheel this afternoon.

### Wednesday, July 19.

In the morning took in lee fore-topmast studding sail. Lat. 17°20′ N. Wind N and E. Course W by S ½ S. At 7 A.M. set fore-royal and -topgallant sail.

### Thursday, July 20.

During the morning unbent fore-topgallant sail and in the afternoon rebent it after having mended it. Wind N and E. Course W by S. At midnight crossed the meridian of longitude and began east longitude. Lat. 16°40′ N.

### Friday, July 21–Saturday, July 22.

Unbent foresail in the morning and repaired it, after which we rebent it. Owing to some process that I do not comprehend, today becomes Saturday in consequence of our having crossed the meridian. Wind N and E. Course W by S ½ S. At 3 P.M. set fore-royal and -topgallant sail.

### Sunday, July 23.

Wind hauled to S and E; took in starboard studding sails. Course W by S ½ S. Had codfish for dinner! ! ! !

### Monday, July 24.

Squared yards and set studding sails both sides. Wind E. Course W by S ½ S. WSW.

Tuesday, July 25.

Lat. 16°21′ N. Long. 171°23′ E. Wind E. Course W by S ½ S. At noon passed a rocky island 20 miles off weather (port) beam, in Lat. 16° N, Long. 171°42 E. Had a fresh mess for dinner.

Wednesday, July 26.

For the last day or two, the wind being at one time aft and at another on the quarter, we have clewed up and set the after sails several times. The weather is getting insufferably hot.

Thursday, July 27.

The Captain gave me the following explanation about east longitude: "In this case, having sailed thus far in west longitude, the ship's time has been the least; but, on crossing the meridian of 180°, it becomes the greatest, and it is necessary to add one to the day of the month. Thus, if you arrive at the meridian on the 21st, as in our case, I call that day the 22d, leaving out the 21st altogether, and using all the corrections for east longitude; the time at the ship will be the greatest and diminish as you proceed to the westward." The jibs and main staysails were set during the night and hauled down again at 7 A.M. Wind hauled to the N and E again during the morning and was very light. Course SW by W ½ W. Average speed 5 knots. Had several rain squalls during the afternoon and evening. Long. 166°12′ E. Lat. 15°23′ N.

Friday, July 28.

Busy making sennit and spun yarn all day long. Long. 163°14′ E. Lat. 14°50′ N. Wind N and E. Course W by S.

Saturday, July 29.

Long. 160°20′ E. Lat. 14°41′ N. Weather very hot.

Sunday, July 30.

Had a very heavy rainsquall at 2 A.M., and, as I had no oil suit on, I got soaked thro'. Lat. 14°54′ N. Long. 157°47′30″ E. Course W. Wind N and E.

**Monday, July 31.**

At 4 A.M. the wind suddenly shifted to NW and blew strong; called all hands to take in studding sails (eleven in number) and, after two hours hard work in the rain, for it poured all night, got them in, the most of them in sad order, being badly ripped. At 7:30 A.M. called all hands again and went about on port tack, steering W by S. Furled royals and set jibs. Weather moderating and the wind hauling aft, made sail. Repaired studding sails and set them. Lat. 14°56′ N.

**Tuesday, August 1.**

Rove new main-topgallant braces and bent main spencer. Wind N and E. Course W ½ S. Lat. 14°56′ N. Long. 153°29 E. Whampoa anchorage bears W 77°51′ N. Dist. 2,328 miles.

**Wednesday, August 2.**

Rove new main-topgallant buntlines and leechlines and fore-topmast-staysail halyards. Chro. Time $5^h 22^m 30^s + 4'51''$. Sun's Alt. 40°37′. Time Watch $3^h$. Lat. 15° N. Long. 151°13′ E. Wind baffling and squally. Course W by S.

## "Our Mess"

### From San Francisco to Hong Kong

Starboard Watch:

> Frank Davis
> E. A. Glover
> W. Clohecy
> C. A. Bouton
> Geo. Savage

Larboard Watch:

> Chas. Bates
> R. Clohecy
> B. K. Burt
> G. L. Packard
> H. M. Gregory

Thursday, August 3.

Rove new mizzen-topgallant buntlines. Busy scraping paintwork between decks and making spun yarn. I cleaned the wheel, a comfortable job. The Captain, talking of bald heads, asked me if Father was not bald and said he remembered the fact from the following occurence: that one day while on deck he happened to take his hat off and no sooner had he done it than a topman dropped a quid of tobacco on top his head, at which there was a great fuss raised. Chro. Time $6^h 1^m 46^s + 4'53''$. Sun's Alt. $33°47'$ Time Watch $4^h$. Lat. $14°46'$ N. Long. $148°31'30''$ E. Whampoa anchorage bears W $75°55'$ N. Dist. 2,055 miles. Wind E. Course W by S. Thermometer $88°$.

Friday, August 4.

At 8 A.M. saw land ahead on starboard bow which proved to be the island of Tinian, lying in Lat. $15°$ N, Long. $145°37'$ E. Soon after, the rest of the Ladrones were in plain sight and could be seen as long as it was light. They were covered with verdure and presented a beautiful appearance. Chro. Time $4^h 21^m 44^s + 4'53''$. Sun's Alt. $59°40'$. Time Watch $2^h$ Lat. $14°54'$ N. Long. $146°19'$ E.

Saturday, August 5.

At midnight a heavy squall struck us, and from 12 to 4 our watch was busy taking in studding sails. An hour later they were all set again and remained so till morning, when, the wind blowing fresh and shifting to SE, they were again taken in and the yards braced around. While taking them in at 12, the weather lower studding sail split from head to foot on the inner leech. At 1 P.M. sent down royal-studding-sail booms. The wind sends us on our way at the rate of 12 knots an hour! At 1:30 P.M. set jibs. At 3 P.M. furled royals, the weather being squally. At 6 P.M. furled fore- and mizzen-topgallant sails and outer jib. Chro. Time $6^h 20^m 39^s + 4'56''$. Sun's Alt. $34°45'$. Time Watch $3^h 40^m$. Lat. $14°52'$ N. Long. $142°27'$ E.

Sunday, August 6.

Heavy rain squalls till 4 A.M. Between 4 and 8 A.M. made sail, set royals, topgallant sails and outer jib. At 3 P.M. set main spencer. Chro.

Time 6ʰ12ᵐ16ˢ + 4′58″. Sun's Alt. 40°36′. Time Watch 3ʰ20ᵐ. Lat. 15°6′ N. Long. 138°35′ E. At 5 P.M. brailed up main spencer. At 7 P.M., weather squally and rainy, furled outer jib and royals.

Monday, August 7.

A squally day. At 4 A.M. the fore-topmast-studding-sail yard (the sail having been set towards midnight) tore a hole in the leech of the foresail, while taking it in. At 5 A.M. set outer jib. At 7 A.M. unbent the weather yardarm of the foresail and repaired the damage, after which it was rebent and set. At 12, a heavy rain squall striking us, clewed up fore- and mizzen-topgallant sails and hauled down outer jib, all of which were reset after the squall passed over. At 1 P.M. set main spencer. For the last two or three days the *Sea Serpent* has done herself justice, going on an average 10 knots per hour. Wind S. Course W. The wind increasing, at 5 P.M. furled topgallant sails and outer jib. At 6 set reefed spanker, wind SSW. At 7:30 P.M., wind still increasing, called all hands to shorten sail, double-reefed topsails and stowed the remains of the inner jib, which had split from clew to earing. Passed the reef earing on lee mizzen-topsail yardarm for the first time. During the morning sent down main-topmast-studding-sail booms and unrove all the gear, fore and aft.

Tuesday, August 8.

Blowing a gale. At 11 A.M., a heavy squall striking us, called all hands to shorten sail; close-reefed topsails and reefed fore- and main courses, after which they were furled. Early in the morning the starboard watch bent a new jib. At 4 P.M. took both quarter boats inboard. At 5:30 furled mizzen topsail. At 10 P.M. called all hands and furled fore-topsail.

Wednesday, August 9.

Gale continues. At 6 A.M. sent down main-topgallant-studding-sail booms and set reefed foresail. Heavy squalls and high sea all day. At 2 P.M., the weather moderating a little, set close-reefed fore-topsail and sent down fore-topgallant-studding-sail booms. The gale has now lasted two days and as yet there are no signs of its breaking. At 7:30 P.M., heavy squalls (accompanied by most vivid lightning, but without rain) striking us, called all hands to shorten sail and furled fore-topsail. At 11:30 P.M., wind abating, set close-reefed fore-topsail.

## Thursday, August 10.

The night was clear and dry. Weather more moderate. During the middle watch set close-reefed mizzen topsail and reefed mainsail. At 7 A.M. set reefed spanker. At 10 A.M. set inner jib and shook the reef out of the mainsail. At 1 P.M., a squall coming on us, furled the spanker. At 3 P.M. sent down royals yards and shook a reef out of main topsail. The sea was high all day, tho' the wind was abating. At 3:30 P.M. shook the reef out of the foresail. Lat. 16°40′ N. Long. 129°27′ E.

## Friday, August 11.

At 4 A.M. shook a reef out of fore-topsail and set main-topgallant sail. At 8 A.M. shook a reef out of main and mizzen topsails. At 10 A.M. unbent the crossjack. The day was beautiful, and a SSW wind sent us on a W by N ½ N course at the rate of 9 knots per hour. At 7:30 P.M., drawing near land and the weather looking threatening, called all hands to shorten sail, furled main-topgallant sail and double-reefed main topsail. Lat. 17°27′ N. Long. 125°46′ E.

## Saturday, August 12.

During the morning watch from 4 to 8 A.M. made sail; shook all the reefs out of topsails and set topgallant sails and outer jib. At day-light saw land on larboard bow which proved to be the Babuyan Is-lands, at the entrance to the China Sea, extending from Lat. 19°1′ to 19°28′ N, and from Long. 121°10′ to 122°12′ E. At 10 A.M. saw a sail on starboard bow and kept gradually overhauling it all day. Toward evening the wind died away, and we were becalmed all night, a NE current setting us inshore. At 8 P.M. brailed main spencer.

## Sunday, August 13.

All day long we were in sight of land, our sails flapping lazily against the masts, as we rose and fell with the swell. Sometimes a light breeze would spring up and enable us just to hold our own. The sail which we saw yesterday (the *Coeur de Lion*, so the Captain said) lay about 6 miles astern of us at noon. Another sail was just in sight off our starboard beam all day, tho' so far off that we could not make out what she was. The *Coeur de Lion*, which sailed from Boston a month before we sailed, ought to have been further on her way than she is, and not have allowed us to overhaul her. The sun was intensely hot and at times, when not a breath of air was stirring, absolutely scorching. Chro. Time $7^h56^m + 4'58''$. Sun's Alt. $32°9'$. Time Watch $4^h$. Lat. $19°44'$ N. Long. $121°34'$ E. At 8 P.M. set weather fore studding sails.

Monday, August 14.

At daylight only one sail could be seen astern (a breeze having sprung up during the night), and many were the speculations as to whether it was the *Coeur de Lion* or not. Finally all doubts were put to an end by Howard's reporting a sail, from the main-topgallant yard, off our port beam, which there was no doubt was her. He probably stood more to the S so as to avoid the mortification of a beating. The breeze freshening, we soon began to show our heels to the vessel astern of us. Instead of washing down, we scrubbed the paintwork on the poop and the other watch finished the main deck by noon, so that we begin to look bright again for port. At 3 P.M. the *Coeur de Lion* was about 10 miles ahead of us off our port bow. Probably by altering her course she avoided the force of the currents which we were all day struggling against. Wind NE. Course W. Chro. Time $7^h25^m40^s + 5'$. Sun's Alt. $40°29'$. Time Watch $2^h$. Lat. $19°23'$ N. Long. $120°9'$ E.

Tuesday, August 15.

During the forenoon watch from 8 to 12 shackled the cables to the anchors and sent up weather main-topgallant-studding-sail booms and set the sail. At noon, the wind beginning to haul ahead, took in all the studding sails. All day long not a sail could be seen, neither of the ships we have been in company with for the last day or so being in sight. During the afternoon scraped the masts and touched up the paintwork on deck. Chro. Time $6^h46^m43^s + 5'2''$. Sun's Alt. $57°32'$. Time Watch $2^h40^m$. Lat. $19°11'$ N. Long. $118°2'$ E.

Wednesday, August 16.

About 2 A.M. the wind died away, and we were totally becalmed (the sea being as smooth as glass and the sun's heat overpowering) till noon, when light and baffling head winds sprang up and lasted all day. Some of the crew went in swimming during the morning, but I did not for fear of sharks, several of which were seen around the ship soon afterwards. Busy all day scrubbing the ship's sides. At 3 P.M. called all hands and went about on starboard tack, steering WSW. Chro. Time $6^h47^m47^s + 5'3''$. Sun's Alt. $51°58'$. Time Watch $2^h40^m$. Lat. $19°41'$ N. Long. $117°8'$ E.

Thursday, August 17.

At 2 A.M. called all hands and went about on port tack, steering NW. At daylight a sail was in sight off the port bow which the Captain said was a schooner, and which was soon out of sight. Busy all the morning scrubbing the ship's sides and bending a new foresail. At 8 P.M. called all hands again and went about on starboard tack, steering SSW. Chro. Time $7^h12^m17^s + 5'5''$. Sun's Alt. $46°46'$. Time Watch $3^h$. Lat. $20°28'$ N. Long. $116°24'$ E.

Friday, August 18.

At 12:30 A.M. called all hands and went about on port tack, steering WNW. An amusing incident occurred while going about, worthy of note. When the order "Topsail haul" was given, Billy, instead of letting go the crossjack braces, kept all fast except the topsail brace; and when Mr. Larrabee sung out, "What's the matter with those crossjack braces? Why don't you do as I tell you?" Billy, with the innocence peculiar to Irish ignorance, sings out, "I thought you said 'Topsail haul,' sir." Whereupon those within hearing distance had a jolly laugh. While washing down decks we had a row with the Chinamen, Harry knocking one of them over the head with a bucket. Soon after a whole crowd of them got ready for a rush on him, which was prevented by the rest of the watch making their appearance on the scene of action, each armed with a handspike. Stacking arms, the mate held a parley with them which ended in his telling them "to go to the D——l" and the crew shaking their handspikes, when John China-man, believing with Shakespeare that "discretion is the better part of valor," beat a hasty retreat. During the morning and till 1 P.M. we were getting up chain cables. At 12 saw several sail which proved to be Chinese junks and sampans. At 12:30 P.M. a sampan came alongside, and we took a pilot aboard (a Chinaman, shoeless and hatless). At 1 P.M. land was to be seen on the starboard bow, and at 3:30 P.M. twelve islands could be counted, which the Captain said were about 21 miles from Hong Kong. During the afternoon got both anchors over the bows and overhauled the range forward of the windlass.

Saturday, August 19.

At 4 A.M. a violent squall struck us; let go everything and clewed up topsails and topgallant sails, after which we wore ship and stood out seaward till the squall passed over, when we made all sail for port. It rained hard and the wind was light, first on one quarter and then on the other, so that we were humbugging all the time. At 2 P.M., a 3-knot current being against us, the wind having died away and being close inshore, dropped anchor. At 7 P.M., it breezing up, weighed anchor but were obliged to drop it again in about an hour, the current being too strong to stem. After dropping anchor we clewed up everything and set anchor watches. The *Coeur de Lion* was becalmed all day about 5 miles ahead of us.

Sunday, August 20.

At 5 A.M. called all hands and weighed anchor but were obliged to drop it again almost immediately. About 7 a violent thunderstorm passed over us. At 8 weighed anchor for the third time and were again compelled to drop it a short time after weighing it. The scenery where we lay is beautiful, high green islands encompassing us on all sides, and on all sides are to be seen sampans, with their little sails made of matting, skimming alongshore. Occasionally, too, a waterspout is to be seen to windward. Such humbugging I never saw before and never want to see again. Up anchor and down anchor, brace up sharp to starboard and, almost before we get the braces belayed, brace up to port, etc., is the order of the day. At 3 P.M. weighed anchor, a breeze having sprung up, and, when opposite a small settlement situated in a pleasant little cove, partly English and partly Chinese, missed stays and, trying to wear, the current being very strong against us, were obliged to drop anchor in order to make her come to the wind; after which we weighed it for the fifth time and stood on starboard tack. At 9 P.M., the breeze being good but not strong enough to enable us to stem the current, clewed up courses and topgallant sails and came to anchor about 3 miles astern of the place we started from. We are only about 10 miles from Hong Kong and yet can't get in.

Monday, August 21.

Laid at anchor till 6 P.M., when an English steamer came down and took us in tow. We furled sails and made everything snug, coming up. At 9:30 P.M. we dropped anchor about a mile from Victoria Town.

Tuesday, August 22.

Busy clearing up after the Chinamen, who all left early in the morning. Sampans were alongside all day with fruit, comprising bananas, pineapples and apples, which were eagerly bought up by all hands. The sun was intensely hot, and awnings were spread over the poop and forecastle.

Wednesday, August 23.

Commenced to paint ship. During the night, it coming on to blow, we were routed out to pay out more chain.

Thursday, August 24.

Painting ship. Had liberty all day. Drew $50 of the Captain and went on board the *Susquehanna* and got the silver for it from Purser Barry. When coming off I went around and looked at the different men-of-war laying at anchor, viz: four American and three English.

Friday, August 25.

Painting ship. Sent down the starboard mainstay, which had stranded, and, after splicing it, set it up again. At 3 P.M. the bark *Merlin* of Boston came alongside and began to discharge her cargo, consisting of cotton drilling in bales, into us, to be taken to Shanghai, whither we are ordered by the agents.

**Saturday, August 26.**

Early in the morning the *Macedonian* came in from Manila and anchored astern of us.

**Sunday, August 27.**

Had liberty in the afternoon and went on board the *Susquehanna* and gave Father's letter of introduction. Found among her officers some old acquaintances, viz: Lieuts. J. Hogan Brown and J. K. Duer. After staying there about an hour I went on board the *Macedonian* for a few minutes and looked all thro' her, after which I came on board. The *Mississippi*, Commodore Perry's flagship, came in at noon and anchored ahead of the *Susquehanna*.* The following is a list of the men-of-war in port (American), viz: *Mississippi, Susquehanna, Powhatan, Macedonian, John Hancock, Vincennes, Porpoise* and the surveying schooner, *J. Fenimore Cooper*; also storeship *Supply*.

**Monday, August 28.**

Busy preparing for sea, putting on chafing gear, etc. During the day several vessels came in, among them the English clipper *David Harrison* and the *Joshua Bates* of New York. In the afternoon the *Merlin* left us.

**Tuesday, August 29.**

At 9 A.M. the *John Hancock* and *J. F. Cooper* sailed. Busy all day overhauling windlass, gypsies and brace blocks.

**Wednesday, August 30.**

Busy all day overhauling sheet sheaves in yardarms, scraping gun carriages and bolts between decks.

**Thursday, August 31.**

After breakfast, discharged sixty bars of quicksilver and ten kegs of butter and then hove short on cable. At 11 A.M. weighed anchor and

* On March 31, 1854, Commodore Perry and the shogun of Japan had concluded the treaty marking the end of Japan's isolation from the West—*Ed*.

stood out to sea by Lyeemoon Pass under all sail. At 1 P.M. no wind, dropped anchor. At 2 P.M. light breezes, weighed anchor, which we were obliged to drop again at 3 P.M., the wind dying away. At 4 P.M. weighed anchor, which we dropped for the third time at 5:30 P.M. At 6:30 P.M. got supper, clewed up and clewed down fore and aft and set anchor watches. The *Stephen Baldwin* of Philadelphia lay at anchor just ahead of us. The pilot said we were about 6 miles from Hong Kong.

Friday, September 1.

At 3:30 A.M. called all hands and got under weigh and stood out to sea. Exchanged signals with a large ship, bound in. At 9 A.M. catted the anchor. At 10 A.M. saw a ship outside, about 10 miles distant. Thro'-out the whole day there was little wind and we were humbugging with the braces the whole time.

Saturday, September 2.

Early in the morning several rainsqualls passed over us. At 8 A.M. exchanged signals with the *Andes* of Boston, off our starboard quarter about 6 miles distant. During the morning got both anchors on the bows and stowed 30 fathoms of each cable in the locker, leaving 45 on deck. At noon the *Andes*'s topgallant masts could just be seen astern of us. Towards night the wind began to increase. At 3 P.M. the outer jib parted; hauled it down and stowed it. At 4 P.M. called all hands, furled topgallant sails and stood by topsail halyards, heavy squalls passing over us. At 6:30 P.M. called all hands and went about on starboard tack. The wind increasing, double-reefed the fore- and main topsails and single-reefed the mizzen. At 11:30 P.M. put another reef in the mizzen topsail and furled the inner jib and set the main spencer.

Sunday, September 3.

At 3 A.M. called all hands to shorten sail, close-reefed fore- and main topsails and furled the mainsail. At daylight saw a sail on the lee bow which passed astern of us, on the port tack, 3 miles distant. She was a clipper ship, showing the American flag, under shortened sail, close-reefed topsails, reefed mainsail, whole foresail, jib and spanker. At 8 A.M. saw two sail on our weather bow which proved to be two sam-

13. *Game Cock*, extreme clipper ship built at East Boston, 1850. This vessel was anchored off Shanghai when the *Sea Serpent* arrived there on September 16, 1854. (Photo of oil painting by Charles Robert Patterson. The Mariners Museum)

14. *Coeur de Lion*, medium clipper ship, built at Portsmouth, New Hampshire, 1854. Gregory visited on board this vessel in San Francisco on June 22, 1854, and the *Sea Serpent* met her at sea a number of times. This ship was also at Shanghai when the *Sea Serpent* arrived there on September 16. (Oil painting by Chong Qua. Smithsonian Institution)

15. *Surprise*, clipper ship built at East Boston, 1850, for the China trade. She arrived at Shanghai on October 6, 1854, and anchored astern of the *Sea Serpent*. (Photo of oil painting by Charles Robert Patterson. The Mariners Museum)

16. Hong Kong harbor. (Gouache print. The Mariners Museum)

17. Hong Kong harbor, ca. 1865. Three British barracks ships are in the foreground. (Tempera drawing. The Mariners Museum)

Lexington  Susquehannah  Powhattan  Macedonian  Mississippi  Vandalia  Saratoga  Southampton  Supply

18. Commodore Perry's fleet in Hong Kong, ca. 1854. Gregory saw some of these vessels during his stay in Hong Kong and boarded the *Susquehanna* and the *Macedonian* on August 27, 1854. (Oil painting. The Mariners Museum)

POWHATAN

19. U.S. Navy sloop-of-war *Powhatan*, built at Norfolk, 1850. Gregory reported seeing this ship at Hong Kong with other vessels of Commodore Perry's fleet on August 27, 1854. (Photo of a painting made in China, 1859. The Mariners Museum)

20. Shanghai harbor, ca. 1865. (Tempera painting. The Mariners Museum)

21. Shanghai harbor. (Tempera painting. The Mariners Museum)

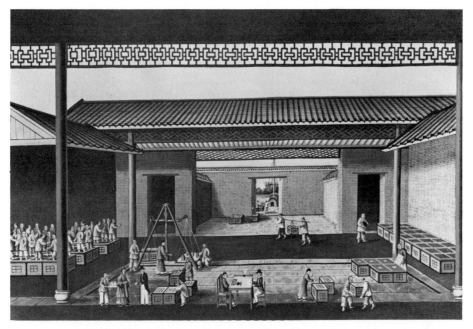

22. American merchants buying tea. Chinese workmen are stamping down tea in chests, weighing, packing and marking chests of tea, and loading them on junk. (Watercolor attributed to Tinqua, who painted in Canton, 1840–70. The Mariners Museum)

23. Wuhsien junk at anchor waiting for the tide in order to sail, Shanghai. The small boat departing from her is loaded with tea. (Watercolor. The Mariners Museum)

24. U.S. Navy man-of-war *Vandalia*, built in Philadelphia, 1825. Her boats transported passengers to the *Sea Serpent* before the latter departed from Shanghai, November 4, 1854. (Lithograph from *Harper's Weekly*, 1861. The Mariners Museum)

pans. Also set reefed spanker. At 8:30 A.M., the wind being steady, wore ship and stood on port tack; also set mainsail and inner jib. The two sampans were in plain sight about ⅛ mile off our port beam, staggering thro' the waves, sometimes hardly visible when they sank in the hollow of a wave. The wind was very high and the sea also.

Monday, September 4.

About 1 A.M. a heavy squall struck the ship on her lee bow, throwing everything aback and forcing her to windward. Called all hands, squared after yards in order to bring her to the wind, after which we braced up on the same tack as before and shortened sail, furled spanker, main spencer and jib, and hauled up the courses. We then wore ship and stood on starboard tack. The rain was incessant and the night pitch dark. At 4 A.M. it stopped raining and the wind moderated. Between 4 and 8 A.M. made sail, set courses, shook two reefs out of main and one out of fore- and mizzen topsails and set main-topgallant sail and inner jib. Between 8 A.M. and 12 noon shook remaining reefs out of topsails and set fore- and mizzen-topgallant sails and spanker, after which we unbent the outer jib, bent a new one and set it. At 1 P.M. called all hands and went about on port tack, being almost becalmed, so soon have all traces of the gale vanished. As the wind has been from the N and E ever since we started, which is a head wind for us, I was not so very much amazed when I found that our latitude was 21°45′ N, considerably to leeward of Hong Kong. Furled the main spencer after going about. We were becalmed, not a breath of air stirring.

Tuesday, September 5.

At 3 A.M. a SW breeze sprang up and we were enabled to head our course, NE by N. The starboard watch rove the fore-lower and -topmast-studding-sail gear and set the weather topmast studding sail. At 8 set lower fore studding sail. This is probably the monsoon which has not yet broken up. Quantities of fish were seen all day long and also several land birds were hopping about the rigging, rather a strange circumstance, considering that we are in blue water. I noticed lately, every once in a while, a large glutinous white body, roundish in shape, float by. I never saw them till we got into the China seas and wonder what they are. I also saw a crab on the surface, live and kicking.

Wednesday, September 6.

Hove the lead several times during the morning watches from 12 to 8 A.M., depth of water varying from 15 to 30 fathoms. At daylight got the weather main-topgallant-studding-sail boom up, rove gear and set the sail. During the morning several sail were in sight, two on our weather and three on our lee quarter. The former proved to be sampans; the latter, two steamers and a schooner. The steamers were in sight all day, passing ahead of us, and from their size were supposed to be two naval steamers (American) which were to sail a few days after us for Monda, one of the Japan Islands. Land was in sight.

Thursday, September 7.

At daylight, off the starboard beam, what proved to be the island of Formosa was seen. Some parts of the island were very high, others quite low, tho' we were so far off that we could only make out the general outline of it. The sunrise was beautiful, more so than usual. Saw a booby, the first one that I have seen in the China seas. The Captain says that the two vessels that were seen yesterday, which we all thought were steamers, were the *Susquehanna* having the *Vincennes* in tow. The wind began to haul to the S and E during the first watch, between 12 and 4 A.M. Courses varying from NE by E to NE by N. At 8 A.M. set lee fore lower and -topmast studding sails and squared yards. At 12 noon sent up port main-topgallant-studding-sail boom; rove gear and set the sail. A ship was in sight off our starboard quarter during the afternoon. Lat. 25°46′ N. Average speed 4½ knots per hour. Evening calm. At sunset hauled down all the studding sails.

Friday, September 8.

When we came on deck at 12 midnight, a heavy thundershower accompanied by the most vivid lightning I ever saw passed over us. The wind came by puffs, from all quarters of the compass; clewed up topgallant sails, hauled down jibs and hauled up the mainsail. We were at the braces all the time, humbugging, bracing first on one tack, then

on the other. At daylight, however, the wind was steady from the N
and E; set topgallant sails, mainsail and jibs. At 7:30 A.M. called all
hands and went about on starboard tack, heading NW. At 12 noon set
main spencer. Busy all the morning scraping royal yards; also unrove
main-topgallant-studding-sail gear. At 1 P.M. sent down main-topgallant-studding-sail booms. At 4 P.M. called all hands and went about on
port tack, heading ESE. At the same time saw land off our port bow,
which proved to be the islands of Pih-Ki-Shan. At 11:45 P.M. called
all hands and went about on starboard tack, heading NW. Also brailed
up main spencer. Lat. 27° 11′ N.

Saturday, September 9.

   At 6 A.M. called all hands and went about on port tack, heading E
by N. At 6 P.M. called all hands and went about on starboard tack,
heading NW.

Sunday, September 10.

   At 2 A.M. called all hands and went about on port tack, heading E
by N ½ N. At 9 A.M. called all hands and went about on starboard
tack, heading NW. This is too bad, a splendid breeze but dead ahead!
Schools of porpoise were playing about the ship all the afternoon. At
8 P.M. called all hands and went about on port tack, heading ESE.

Monday, September 11.

   At 8 A.M. called all hands and went about on starboard tack, heading NW. For the last two or three days the wind has varied from N
to NE. Heavy squalls were forming to leeward of us during the morning. Busy all day cleaning muskets and sabers. At 3 P.M. a Chinese junk
was in sight, which we passed at 4:30 P.M. The Captain said she was
a pirate, and he was in a terrible fluster; got up his rifle, examined the
ship's arms, etc. At 5 P.M. saw land ahead which proved to be the
islands of Chu San, laying in Lat. 30° 1′ N and Long. 122° 6′ E. While
looking at them, I saw a whale spout and shortly after saw part of his
body. Jim Melville, who has been whaling, told me it was a finback.
At 8 P.M. called all hands and went about on port tack, heading E.

Tuesday, September 12.

At 4 A.M. called all hands and went about on starboard tack, heading NW. The wind began to die away, and all the morning our sails were flapping, hardly air enough stirring to fill them. A heavy swell from the E set in during the night and continued all day. At 12:30 P.M. braced around on port tack. The bolt that supports the slings of the main yard having drawn, Mr. Cornell secured it by a preventer sling of a hawser, so that in case the bolt should draw entirely, the weight of the yard would not come on the lifts alone. The wind springing up from the N and E again, called all hands at 3:30 P.M. and went about on starboard tack, heading NW. At 7 P.M. called all hands and went about on port tack, steering E. During the evening the wind hauled due E, and at 10 P.M. braced around on starboard tack, heading her course N by E.

Wednesday, September 13.

At daylight saw land off port beam and ahead which proved to be the islands—Four Sisters, Two Brothers—Lucona and Barren. At 9 A.M. squared in yards a little and set weather fore-topmast studding sail. At 10 A.M. the Saddle Islands were in sight, 10 miles distant on our lee bow. During the afternoon passed these islands, also Parker Islands; squared in yards; at 4 P.M. steered due W and set a jack at the fore for a pilot. Several fishing boats and a ship were also in sight. Also got both anchors over the bows. The sail proved to be the *Tinqua*, Whitmore of Philadelphia, homeward bound. She passed about a mile astern of us in fine style. At 6 P.M. took in studding sails. At 7 P.M. called all hands to shorten sail; furled topgallant sails, courses, jibs, and clewed topsails, and at 8:15 P.M. dropped anchor in 6 fathoms of water.

Thursday, September 14.

At daylight got under weigh and stood in with a stiff breeze. The water was a muddy yellow, from which circumstance I presumed we were in a part of the Yellow Sea. Kept a man in chains all the time, the water varying from 3 to 5 fathoms. At 10 A.M. saw the mainland, two ships ashore and a steamer assisting them. At 11:30 A.M. took a pilot on board. At 3 P.M. dropped anchor about 6 miles from Wuhsien.

At night the Captain went up to Shanghai to get a steamer. Went on sick list, having a blood boil on my knee.

Friday, September 15.

Overhauling blocks and repairing service on rigging.

Saturday, September 16.

At 6 A.M. a heavy thundershower passed over us. At 6:30 A.M. the Captain returned with a towboat and took us in tow. The scenery as we passed up the river was magnificent. A verdure only known in tropical climates clothed the banks in green, while here and there a hut could be seen peeping from beneath a cluster of bushes and trees. The rice fields too, along the banks in various states of cultivation, added interest to the scene. Then, too, in bends of the river were ship-yards with junks on the stocks. We passed also several fleets of junks, one of which numbered at least two or three hundred, anchored in lines as close together as possible, all waiting for the monsoon. At 10 A.M. moored off Shanghai. During the afternoon got up awnings and stripped off chafing gear. We were moored between two Chinese men-of-war, a bark and brig, flying the rebel flag.* Coming in contact with the brig, we were obliged to unship our spanker boom. A heavy cannonading was heard in the direction of the upper city, which, the peddlers that came off told us, was the rebels firing upon the imperial encampment from the other side of the river. Ahead of us lays a French war steamer, the *Colbert*, while in a rude kind of a dry dock about ⅛ mile from our anchorage is the *Jeanne d'Arc*, a 74-gun ship, repairing, having been ashore. One of her crew was aboard of us; he said that the allied fleets were before Lt. Petersburgh, quite a piece of news for us. We found laying at anchor the clipper ships: *Game Cock*, *Messenger*, *Union*, *Panama* and *Coeur de Lion*, the latter having made the run from Hong Kong in eight days.

Sunday, September 17.

A rainy day. Stayed aboard all day. During the evening the French steamer's band played most beautifully till quite late. From there be-

---

* At this time China was in the midst of the Taiping Rebellion, led by Hung Hsiu-ch'üan, whose goal was to set up a new dynasty. The rebels had captured Nanking in 1853 and had made it their capital—*Ed.*

ing no firing, I presume there was a cessation of hostilities between the belligerent parties.

Monday, September 18.

During last night the *Ariel*, *Jenny Pitts* and *Andes* came in. During the day unbent all three topgallant sails, foresail and jibs, and struck fore- and main-topgallant masts so as to overhaul the eyes of the rigging, which was sent down on deck. A heavy cannonading was kept up all day. Rainy.

Tuesday, September 19.

All last night there was a heavy cannonading, mostly from the city; the batteries were so near that we could see the flash every time. Busy all day overhauling topgallant rigging. Rainy weather.

Wednesday, September 20.

Raining again; they say that the rainy season is just setting in. Began to discharge cargo, cotton drilling. The mate gave me a good billet, viz: to take account of them. The Chinese men-of-war were firing nearly all day at boats that were running the blockade, but with little success, for I believe after all no one was hurt.

Thursday, September 21.

Rained hard all day. The men were busy between decks repairing sails, while we boys, for want of a better job, were sent down into the hold to pound the stream chain.

Friday, September 22.

A beautiful day. Discharging cargo. During the day sent up fore-topgallant mast and set up forestays and backstays. Also sent down main-topmast stay.

Saturday, September 23.

Set up fore topgallant rigging and overhauled main-topgallant rigging and topmast stay; unbent sails and finished taking out cotton drilling.

Sunday, September 24.

Had liberty all day. Jim and myself started off about 9 A.M. on a regular cruise, to see everything that could be seen. First I went on board the *Andes* to see Ned Devens, whom I found well and jolly as ever. After leaving the *Andes* we went all over the city, that is, the European part of it, for the Chinese city is in ruins. I was glad enough to get aboard again towards evening, for the streets were so very filthy and the Chinamen such a miserable-looking set of beings that one soon got disgusted with the shore. At noon the *Coeur de Lion* left for New York with 1,500 tons of tea on board.

Monday, September 25.

Discharged all the quicksilver, 500 flasks. Sent up main-topmast stay before breakfast instead of washing down decks. During the rest of the day set up forestay and main-topmast stay, sent up main-topgallant mast and set up the backstays and rigging.

Tuesday, September 26.

Began to discharge ballast. During the morning sent up fore- and main-topgallant yards. At noon H. M. Steamer *Rattler* came in and dropped anchor near us, after which she saluted the French admiral, which was returned by the *Colbert*.

Wednesday, September 27.

Discharging ballast and clearing out the hold to get ready for cargo.

Thursday, September 28.

Discharging ballast; painted masts and fore-topgallant yard. Also scraped fore-topgallant-studding-sail booms and sent them up. The *Powhatan* arrived during the afternoon and anchored ahead of us.

Friday, September 29.

Finished discharging ballast and painted topmast heads.

Saturday, September 30.

Scrubbed copper, sent up main-topgallant-studding-sail booms and main-topsail tie and sheet, which had been ashore for a day or so repairing. In the afternoon took in 581 chests of Twankay tea. Mr. Larra-bee gave me the chopsticks to take charge of, a good job, which will last all the time we are here.

Sunday, October 1.

Was ashore all day. During the morning Jim and myself tried to get into the city, but just as we got to the gates we heard a loud report from the imperialist camp, which was followed by a Whiz! right over our heads and a bang just inside the walls that told us the ball had done its errand, and we retreated. During the morning I presented my letters of introduction to Russell & Co., seeing Mr. Cunningham, who was most polite, offering me a horse at 5 o'clock and giving me an invite to dinner at 7, the latter of which I accepted. Going, I spent a most pleasant evening, meeting at dinner Judge McLane, the American commissioner, Mr. Murphy, the consul, and his lady and Mr. C. A music box which was the finest I ever saw and which cost $1,500 played most exquisitely during a great part of the evening. About 10 P.M. I returned on board, glad enough to get back again.

Monday, October 2.

Took in 851 half chests of Gunpowder tea and 445 half chests of Imperial from consignees marked TSH.

Tuesday, October 3.

Got up the water casks and cleaned them. Also took in 177 quarter chests of Gunpowder, 200 half chests of Imperial and 1,283 half chests of Young Hyson teas from consignees marked TSH.

Wednesday, October 4.

Took in 163 quarter chests of Young Hyson and 1,641 half chests. Also painted the water casks and lashed them in their places. H.B.M. Sloop-of-War *Racehorse* sailed during the afternoon.

Thursday, October 5.

Took in 326 half chests of Young Hyson Tea. TSH.

Friday, October 6.

Was up at the mizzen-topgallant head scraping off the white paint from 10 A.M. till 5:30 P.M. preparatory to varnishing it. The 2d mate was busy all the morning getting preventer slings fitted to the main yard. The clipper ship *Surprise* came in during the afternoon and anchored astern of us.

Saturday, October 7.

Early in the morning the clipper ship *Golden Gate* came in and anchored below us. Had liberty all day and went all over the city. The Chinese city is mostly in ruins, having been bombarded so long; but the European part is beautiful. Large houses built in a style peculiar to the place, and mostly surrounded by elegant gardens, give a stylish and rather an imposing look to the city as you approach it. The city is ruled by the three powers, American, French and English, who have control of the customhouse and who, in company with a Chinese consul, make any laws necessary to govern the place. The money collected at the customhouse is to be given to the party that come out conquerors in the present civil struggle. During the afternoon the steamer *John Hancock* came in. A rumor is afloat that the *Powhatan*, *Rattler* and *Colbert* are going up to Peking to have an audience with the emperor to demand satisfaction for injuries committed to European inhabitants of Shanghai by the troops before the city; and that in case of a refusal the allied powers intend to drive the imperialists away.

Sunday, October 8.

Stayed aboard all day. The *J. Fenimore Cooper* came in during the morning.

Monday, October 9.

Scraped gratings, belaying pins, etc. Also washed the ship's side. My chum Jim went on the sick list.

Tuesday, October 10.

At 2 P.M. the *Powhatan* got under weigh and went down the river, bound for Peking or Nanking. An hour later the *John Hancock*, having the *J. Fenimore Cooper* in tow, and H.B.M. Steam Frigate *Rattler* also started for the same place. Cleaned and oiled the copper at the water's edge.

Wednesday, October 11.

Pounded shank painters and ring stoppers, scraped belaying pins, etc.

Thursday, October 12.

Filled up some of the water casks.

Friday, October 13.

Cleaned out boys' rooms and the forecastle.

Saturday, October 14.

Filled the remainder of the water casks and scraped the masts. The British clipper *Crest of the Wave* sailed during the afternoon. Bishop Boone came on board in the morning, and I must say I was disappointed in the looks of the man, for a more stuck-up looking personage I think I never fell in with before.

Sunday, October 15.

Went on shore for a couple of hours in the morning. The *Jenny Pitts* sailed at noon.

Monday, October 16.

Got up all the spare water casks, empty bread barrels, etc., from between decks and were busied filling them till late.

Tuesday, October 17.

Thank gracious, we got thro' with the water, everything being full that could possibly hold water.

Wednesday, October 18.

Busy holystoning hatches, scraping gratings, etc. A very hot day.

Thursday, October 19.

Holystoning hatches, scraping grating and paint pots.

Friday, October 20.

A cold blustering day. The *Ariel* sailed at noon.

Saturday, October 21.

Took in 1,714 packages of teas in chests, half chests and 10/c boxes comprising Hyson, Gunpowder and Imperial teas from Russell & Co., being the surplus of the *Panama*'s cargo: marked ⟨H⟩. Also 735 half chests of Hyson, Gunpowder, Twankay and Imperial teas from Wetmore & Co. marked ⟨WW⟩, 342 marked ⌷SWG⌷ and 123 chests marked N/W, making 2,914 packages in all.

Sunday, October 22.

Went ashore in the morning for something I needed; otherwise I think I should never have set foot on shore, for Shanghai offers little inducement to do so. The weather was cold and a double-reef topsail gale blew, so that I had difficulty in getting up to the city, narrowly escaping an upset. After going to Kin Tee-yuen's for some Nankin, I called on Mr. Cunningham to say farewell and then came on board again.

Monday, October 23.

A wintry cold day, woolen clothes being quite desirable for comfort. Busy getting ready for sea, lashing spars, beef and pork barrels, guns, etc., from which I suppose we are to sail soon. Jim Allen left us today and went down to Wuhsien to join the *Ariel* as mate: if he is fit for mate I am for captain, that's all. Took in 452 half chests of Hyson, Gunpowder and Imperial teas, 81 being musters, for Russell & Co., marked ⟨H⟩; 858 half chests from consignees, 200 marked MDC, 418 TSH, and 240 ⟨M⟩; being 1,310 packages in all. Jim seems if anything to be worse. The *Messenger* sailed at noon.

**Tuesday, October 24.**

The *Panama* sailed at noon for New York; as she passed us her crew gave us three cheers and fired her gun as she came abreast of the *Surprise*, both of which salutes were returned. Took in 45 boxes of straw marked ⟨BN⟩ from our consignees, Bull, Nye & Co., also 8 bales of straw marked LSB, 27 DC, 32 boxes LSW, and 6 LSB, 300 bales matting (no mark) from Hanbury and Co., making 418 packages in all. Busy all day getting ready for sea.

**Wednesday, October 25.**

Took in 674 half chests of Twankay, Imperial, Gunpowder and Hyson teas from Augustine Heard & Co., all marked SWG; 642 marked N/W and 221 SWG from Wetmore & Co.; and 123 10/c boxes from consignees marked TSH; making 1,660 packages in all; and 20 cases of silk from Mr. Cobb. The Chinese city of Shanghai was on fire, blazing all day, probably set on fire by the imperialists. During the afternoon set up the fore- and main-royal and -topgallant stays and backstays and jib guys.

**Thursday, October 26.**

Took in 1,010 half chests of Hyson and Twankay teas marked ⟨WW⟩ and 275 N/W from Wetmore & Co.; 668 from Bull, Nye & Co. marked TSH; also 50 cases straw braid marked CB; also 431 half chests tea from Hanbury & Co. marked Ⓡ .

**Friday, October 27.**

Took in 474 packages tea (half chests) marked 385 ⟨C⟩ and 89 ⟨SS⟩. Also 138 cases silks marked, viz: WH/NP WH/L TK/P TK/S from Hanbury & Co.; 336 half chests marked ⟨W & Co.⟩ from Watson & Co.; 467 half chests marked N/W, SWG and ⟨WW⟩ from Wetmore & Co.; and 117 boxes straw braid marked CB from Bull, Nye & Co. Bent courses, topsails, topgallant sails, jibs, spencers, spanker, and crossed royal yards. The *Andes* dropped down abreast of us during the morning, and at noon I went on board of her to see Ned Devens.

Saturday, October 28.

Bent all the studding sails and got the gear ready for use. The *Andes* sailed for Boston during the morning. Took in 100 cases silk marked RB & Co. from Reiss & Co.; 2 cases silk marked ⟨BC⟩ from Beriss & Cobb; 23 bales raw silk marked a/c/b/h from A. Heard & Co.; and 458 half chests of Hyson, Imperial and Gunpowder teas marked SWG from Wetmore & Co.

Sunday, October 29.

Went ashore to Kin Tee-yuen's to get some things for Jim. Also got my camphor chest.

Monday, October 30.

Put on all the chafing gear, fore and aft. Took in 21 bales raw silk marked ⟨FB⟩ from H. Fogg & Co.; 120 boxes straw and 1 box sundries marked CK and ⟨TPC⟩ from Hanbury & Co.; and 3 boxes silk from Wetmore & Co.

Tuesday, October 31.

Sent up a preventer main-topmast stay and bent the staysail on it. Took in 1 box silk marked CWW from W. S. Wetmore.

Wednesday, November 1.

Took in 650 packages of tea (half chests), Hyson, Imperial and Gunpowder, marked KMC from A. Heard & Co., which completed our cargo. At 4 P.M. battened down the main hatches and are at last ready for sea.

Thursday, November 2.

After breakfast hove up port anchor and hove short on starboard one. At 3:30 P.M. hove starboard anchor off bottom and dropped down the river about a mile and a half to a clear anchorage, when we came to anchor, with port anchor out, and hove up and catted the starboard one. The Pilot told us that the *Andes* was ashore near Wuhsien and could not be got off till the next spring tide. Remained at anchor all night.

Friday, November 3.

Remained at anchor all day waiting for the steamer to get her smoke pipe up, which was knocked down several days ago in a collision with the *Surprise*. The principal duty all day was getting the stock, comprising sheep, pigs, ducks, chickens, geese, turkeys and pigeons, in their proper sea quarters, and a most lovely serenade they kept up. Shanghais are all the rage, and for a quarter of a dollar I became the possessor of a rooster which many a "Shanghai fancier" in the States would envy me the possession of.

Saturday, November 4.

At daybreak hove short. At 8 A.M. the passengers, Mrs. Hall, two nurses and three children, and Miss Wray, came on board in the *Vandalia*'s boats; a half hour later the steamer had us in tow, and we soon left Shanghai behind us and were at last homeward bound! Off the bar at Wuhsien the steamer left us and went back while we proceeded on our voyage with all sail set. At 8 P.M., the Pilot wishing to keep on, the Captain gave orders to anchor; furled light sails, clewed up topsails and courses. Soon after, a large English ship passed us within 50 feet of our stern, hailed us, wishing a pleasant voyage to the Captain and sending his compliments to the ladies, whom he knew. Our Captain, I thought, was excessively impolite, never even wishing a pleasant voyage in return, but giving utterance to a species of grunts intended for "Thank you."

Sunday, November 5.

At 5 A.M. (moonlight) all hands were called to man the windlass; weighed anchor and made all sail. At 8 A.M. came to anchor, being unable to stem the tide, the wind being light; an hour later weighed anchor, as I trust for the last time, and stood on our way with a fair fresh breeze. Got the anchors cockbilled, and during the morning set port fore-topgallant and -topmast and main-topgallant studding sails, the latter of which we hauled down at noon. I shall be glad when we leave the Yellow Sea and get into blue water again. At 6 P.M. set main-topgallant studding sail (port). The night was magnificent, the moon being at its full, while the NE monsoon sent us flying on a S course at the rate of 10 knots per hour. During the night took in fore-topgallant studding sail.

Monday, November 6.

During the morning the starboard watch sent up the main-topmast-studding-sail booms and set port lower studdingsail. In the afternoon our watch sent up main-royal-studding-sail booms, rove gear and set the sails, set starboard main-topmast and -topgallant and fore-topmast and lower studding sails, also port topmast studding sail. Lat. 28°3′ N. Speed 8 knots. Course SW. Wind NE. During the day took both anchors in on deck. Blue water again.

Tuesday, November 7.

During the day the wind was strong from the N and E a little off the starboard quarter; took in all port studding sails, also starboard main-topmast studding sail, and set fore-topgallant studding sail. Rove new spanker peak halyards and main-topmast-studding-sail tacks. At 3 P.M. set main spencer, which was brailed up at 7 P.M. At 4 P.M. a group of islands were in plain sight off our starboard bow, the largest of which was Turnabout Island. Speed 10 knots.

Wednesday, November 8.

During the afternoon set port main studding sails. Course SW by W. Speed 10 knots and at times 12.

Thursday, November 9.

A regular stiff breeze all day. During the morning took in all the studding sails and set main spencer. In the afternoon hauled down jibs, brailed up spencer, squared the yards and rigged in all the booms. At 1 P.M. the main-topmast staysail split and was hauled down; also furled mizzen royal. Course SW by W. Speed 11½ knots. Passed several fleets of junks during the day. Lat. 21°15′ N. At 4 P.M. furled mizzen-topgallant sail and fore- and main royals.

Friday, November 10.

A heavy sea, ship rolling lee scuppers under, and of course no comfort to be taken. At 4 A.M. furled crossjack and fore-topgallant sail and set main spencer. Breakers could be seen from the crosstrees, off our weather beam. Speed 10½ knots.

Saturday, November 11.

Still rolling, as if it was fated that we were to roll till we carried away something. Everything in our room gets adrift as often as we lash them, and a pretty mess it is, chests sliding, bottles breaking, etc.; and to eat one has to shovel it in fast as possible, and ten to one he then, in spite of his care, finds himself going headlong, eatables and all, into the adjoining bulkhead. At noon saw a large ship off starboard quarter, close-hauled, being probably bound to San Francisco. At 4 P.M. furled main-topgallant sails, heavy squalls passing over us. At 4:15 P.M. furled mainsail. At 5 P.M. double-reefed mizzen topsail, and at 6 called all hands and double-reefed fore-topsail.

Sunday, November 12.

Same as yesterday, squally. Lat. 9°1′ N. Caught a booby late in the evening on the mizzen-topgallant yardarm; brought him down and kept him tied by one leg, all night. During the afternoon set main-topgallant sail.

Monday, November 13.

During the night the sea and wind having abated, at daylight began to make sail; set mainsail, main royal and fore-topgallant sail, and shook reefs out of fore-topsail. At 9 A.M. brailed up main spencer, shook reefs out mizzen topsail and set the topgallant sail and royal.

At 11 A.M. set fore-royal. During the morning bent main-topmast stay-sail, which had been unbent for the purpose of mending it. At noon set main-topgallant (starboard) and fore lower and -topmast studding sails, the wind being light. Lat. 5°55′ N. Tied the ship's name, date and latitude to the booby I caught last night and let him go. During the afternoon and night it was squally, accompanied by heavy rain, as is always the case in these latitudes; and, as we were drawing near to land, at sunset shortened sail, took in studding sails, furled royal and topgallant sails and hauled up courses.

Tuesday, November 14.

At 4 A.M. hove to and remained so till daylight (making leeway all the time), when we made all sail. At 2 P.M. saw land, a point and a half on starboard bow, and passed it at 6 P.M., steering S by W-SSW. It was the island of Grand, or Great Natuna, extending from Lat. 3°40′ to 4°16′ N, and from Long. 108°11′ to 108°26′ E, and was very high in places while some parts of it extended along just above the horizon. Squally all day, and towards night furled royals and fore- and mizzen-topgallant sails and hauled up mainsail. Lat. 3°37′ N.

Wednesday, November 15.

At 4 A.M., a heavy squall striking us, called all hands to shorten sail; hauled up foresail, double-reefed main topsail and hauled out fore- and mizzen-topsail reef tackles ready to reef when the squall passed and the Captain gave orders to make sail again. Shook the reefs out of main topsail and set all three topsails, fore- and main courses and main-topgallant sail. At 9 A.M. set main royal. During the day quantities of kelp, shells, etc., were floating by, indicating most probably the vicinity of some reef or island ahead of us. It rained incessantly till noon, when it cleared off. At noon set studding sails, the wind being very light. At 2 P.M. set fore-topgallant sail and at 3, the mizzen-topgallant sail. Looking over the side, to my amazement I saw a snake, like an adder in color, swim by, a circumstance those who have been in these seas before tell me is of frequent occurrence. Land was in sight all the afternoon and night off port side, consisting of numerous rocky islands, some of considerable size. Lat. 1°53′ N.

Thursday, November 16.

Almost becalmed. Land in sight, to port, one island being very high and steep, the rest small. All the islands seen yesterday and today comprise a group called Tambelan Islands, extending from Lat. 7' to 2°15' N, and from Long. 105°32' to 108°32' E. Towards night squally; took in light sails. At 10 P.M., a heavy squall passing over us, clewed up everything and stood by topsail halyards. Lat. 46' N. Course S.

Friday, November 17.

At 2 A.M. made all sail again. Almost becalmed, averaging but 3 knots. During the morning set studding sails. At noon squally; took in studding sails, clewed up royals, furling fore- and mizzen, and hauled up foresail. At 2 P.M. a brig passed us bound N. Lat. 48' S. Course S. We crossed the Line this morning 3 A.M. in Long. 107°8' E. At 6 P.M. furled fore-topgallant sail and main royal, almost a total calm. At 11 P.M. braced round sharp on starboard tack, a breeze springing up, steering S. During the day got both anchors over the bows.

Saturday, November 18.

At daylight made all sail again. Squally all day and rainy. Several times hauled up courses and clewed up topgallant sails and royals till the squall passed. This clewing up so often is hard on us, as our watch only consists of eight men and five boys; one man and one boy being sick and the man at the wheel being taken out only leaves ten hands to do the work. The Captain seems to be very careful, not knowing the sea, shortening sail every night and keeping a man aloft to look out for shoals; also heaving the lead often. The winds seem to be peculiar, suddenly shifting from one quarter to another; and by the way the squalls work around, it would seem that the winds are rotary in their movements. At noon a heavy squall struck us; called all hands, furled topgallant sails and royals and hauled up courses. At 1 P.M. saw a sail off starboard beam. At 3 P.M. set courses and main- and fore-topgallant sails. Land was in sight dead ahead which proved to be Gaspar Island, also a large ship. At 4 P.M. land was discovered off the starboard beam which belonged also to the same group, island after island of which rapidly came to view, until no less than a dozen were in sight. At sunset we were fairly in Gaspar Strait and continued to stand on till 10 P.M., when we came to anchor in 20 fathoms water; clewed up everything and set anchor watch. At 11 P.M. a heavy squall struck us; called all hands and made everything snug, hauling up buntlines and topsail clew lines.

Sunday, November 19.

At 5 A.M. got under weigh, all sail set, braced sharp on starboard tack. At 12 P.M. braced round on port tack, very little wind stirring. At 2 P.M. becalmed and, the current setting us towards a reef, dropped anchor and clewed up royals, all hands standing by to get under weigh again whenever a breeze springs up. Land in sight every point, no less than twenty islands being visible, some very large, others little more than reefs, of which these straits are full. Long. 107°11′ E. At 5 P.M., breezing up a little, got under weigh again; but the wind not being very strong, we were obliged to anchor again at 7 P.M.; furled royals and topgallant sails, hauled up courses and clewed down topsails.

Monday, November 20.

At 5 A.M. got under weigh, a light breeze blowing. While weighing anchor and in the act of fleeting jig the chain surged, running out several fathoms and carrying Mr. Lind with it forward of the windlass. For a second I thought it was the last of him, but luckily the chain ceased paying out and we hauled him out. On examination we found that nothing was injured except a bruised ankle; it was a miracle that he was not killed outright, as he would have been had the chain run out a fathom more. The wind being dead ahead, we had a dead beat of it, tacking every two or three hours. At noon, four sail were in sight to leeward of us, two of which were Malay proas and the other two, a bark and a brig. At 4 P.M. saw a column of smoke arising on the horizon, which, the mate said, was a wreck on fire surrounded by proas. At 4:30 one of the heaviest squalls we have had since we left New York struck us; let fly halyards and sheets, fore and aft, and clewed up everything. The wind continued with irresistible force for about ten minutes, when the squall passed to leeward and left us totally becalmed. At 5 made all sail again and continued on.

Tuesday, November 21.

We continued on till at 12:30 A.M. we came to anchor; clewed up and down and set anchor watches. At 4 A.M. got under weigh, all sail set. At 10 A.M. the brig was close to, but, a breeze arising, gradually we forged ahead of her. The wind for the last two or three days has been extremely light and variable, hardly allowing us steerageway at times. Lat. 3°19′ S.

Wednesday, November 22.

Totally becalmed all the morning and until 4 P.M., when a light breeze sprung up; set studding sails. No land was in sight all day, having passed thro' Gaspar Strait and entered the Java Sea. Two proas were in sight all the afternoon. We came thro' Clements Strait, between Bangka and Billiton islands. At 5 P.M. two sail were in sight ahead of us, one of which, a bark, passed us, close-hauled, evidently bound to Calcutta. Lat. 3°54′ S. Course SW.

Thursday, November 23.

At 4 A.M. a heavy thundershower passed over us, accompanied by the loudest thunder and most vivid lightning I ever saw: clewed up everything. At daylight land was in sight which proved to be the Islands of Two Brothers, in Lat. 5°9′ S and Long. 106°3′ E. They were the most beautiful islands I ever saw, being one mass of foliage and rising almost perpendicularly from the water: we passed them at 9 A.M. and came then in full sight of Sumatra off starboard side. Two sail were also in sight, one ahead and the other astern, which was close-hauled, going to Calcutta. Course SW. Speed 8 knots. At 11 A.M. Java was in plain sight, also another sail, a brig, off port beam, steering NE. The sail ahead of us kept gaining on, and the Captain said she was the *Andes*. At 2 P.M. passed between the Button and Java and came in sight of Anjer Lor, and hove to for a boat which was seen coming off to us. The Captain gave orders that no one should trade with it and, when it came alongside, bought everything he had to sell that was worth having, birds, fruit, etc., and then gave orders to fill away, not waiting for four other boats to get alongside so that the men could get a chance to buy. It is always customary for ships to heave to for provisions off Anjer, and, as numbers of boats come off, the men have a chance to get fruit; but the Captain's meanness would not allow them to get anything. Without any exception he is the meanest specimen of humanity I ever saw, and a glutton, for he is always running to the galley to see what's for dinner and makes as much fuss about his fowls as if he had never seen any before, even going so far as to doubt the validity of my claim to my Shanghai. The carpenter and 3d mate got some monkeys, the only thing the Captain's meanness spared. At 8 P.M. passed Java Head, in Lat. 6°48′ S and Long. 105°13′ E, and were thro' the Sunda straits and in the Indian Ocean. Looking squally, furled royals.

Friday, November 24.

At 6 A.M. set main royal. A sail was in sight off port beam. No land in sight. The mate told us while washing decks that the *Coeur de Lion* was forty-three days from Shanghai to Java Head. The 2d steward was the occasion of a regular row; for refusing duty, the Captain tried to tie his hands and was obliged to get the mate, 2d mate and carpenter to assist before he could do it. The Captain asking the mate for irons, received for an answer that there never having been occasion under her former Captain to use them, there were none on board. The Captain was as much to blame as Ben, I think, tho' Ben had no excuse for his impudence. Towards night furled fore- and mizzen royals. Wind SE trades. Course SW by W. Speed 8 knots. The starboard watch stowed both chains in the locker and got port anchor in on deck in the morning, and our watch got the starboard anchor in during the afternoon.

Saturday, November 25.

The trades send us flying on our way, braced sharp on port tack, and will carry us to the Cape, if luck is on our side, without stopping. During the morning stowed stream chain in chain trunk and kedge anchors under the windlass. Wind SE. Course SW by W. Speed 9 knots. Lat. 8°23′ S. In the afternoon the main royal split and was sent down; a new one sent up and bent. Unrove topgallant-studding-sail gear. The Southern Cross is now in plain sight every night. A sail was in sight all the afternoon off the lee bow. At 11:30 P.M. furled royals and set fore- and main spencers.

Sunday, November 26.

Kept gaining all night on the sail ahead till at 5 A.M. she was off our starboard beam about ⅛ mile distant. And a noble sight it was; she had a main skysail and fore-topmast studding sail set and loomed up tremendously in the morning mist. At 5 (daylight) she was so near that we could read her name with the naked eye (making her out to be the clipper ship *Star of Liberty* of New York). She struggled hard to keep up; but at last had the mortification of being dropped by us, under topgallant sails. At 7 A.M. the *Star* being 4 miles astern, set royals and then began to drop her fast, at 2 P.M. she being hull down astern. Course WSW.

Monday, November 27.

In the morning shifted over main topsail halyards and put new ratlines wherever they were needed, on the port lower rigging. Wind SE. Course WSW. Speed 9 knots. Lat. 11°2′ S. At 11 P.M., the wind shifting aft, squared in yards and set starboard fore lower, -topmast and -topgallant and main-topgallant studding sails.

Tuesday, November 28.

At work about decks. At night took in studding sails.

Wednesday, November 29.

During the morning unbent the inner jib and bent an old one in its place; also sent down lee main lift and weather spanker topping lift to be overhauled. At 10 A.M. set fore-topmast and -topgallant studding sails; while swaying up the former, the whip parted, precipitating all hands on deck and injuring Harry Coles, who was on the sail, quite badly, striking his head on the spare jibboom. Charles Bates told me that G. W. Warren, former mayor of Charlestown, is his uncle: he said the one who kept store in Washington St. and believed that they were both the same personage, tho' whether the mayor is proprietor of Warren's I know not. At 4 P.M. set main-topgallant and at 10 P.M. fore lower studding sails. Course WSW ½ W. Speed 9 knots.

Thursday, November 30.

At 9 A.M. unbent foresail and bent an old one in its place. During the afternoon set starboard main-topmast studding sail and at 3 P.M. called all hands and unbent fore-topsail and got up an old one and bent it. During the day, the wind hauling aft a little, brailed up spencers. Lat. 16°46′ S. At 6 P.M. took in main-topmast and fore lower studding sails.

Friday, December 1.

Took everything out of the manhole and, after cleaning the old iron, etc., restowed it. At 4 P.M. a sail was in sight off weather bow. Towards night the wind began to die away and was light all night.

Saturday, December 2.

At daylight squally, wind coming from N and W; took in all studding sails and braced round on starboard tack. The sail we saw ahead last night is astern off our port quarter about 8 miles distant and is a full-rigged ship. Pretty good for us, I think, as everything we have seen, so far, we have passed. At 10 A.M., wind hauling aft, squared yards and set main-topgallant, fore lower and -topmast (port) studding sails. During the afternoon set port fore-topgallant and both main-topmast studding sails. Kept gaining all day on the ship.

Sunday, December 3.

A hot, humbugging day. The ship not in sight at daylight. During the morning light breezes dead aft, set all studding sails except main-royal. While setting main-topmast studding sail, the halyard whip block broke and came down on deck, hitting "Frenchy" on the tip of one of his fingers; the most narrow escape I ever saw, for, had it deviated an inch in its course, it would have knocked seven bells out of him. At noon hauled down all studding sails and braced up sharp on starboard tack; humbugged all day by light winds. Lat. 19°33′ S. Long. 78°8 E. At 12 M. clewed up royals.

Monday, December 4.

Light winds all the morning. At noon, however, a breeze sprang up from the S, braced round sharp on port tack averaging 4 knots per hour, heading W. Finished overhauling topsail yard footropes, which both watches have been busy at for the last day or so. Set royals at 7 A.M. At 2 P.M. set fore- and main spencers. A sail was in sight from main royal at 4 P.M. off our lee quarter.

Tuesday, December 5.

The breeze freshened during the night and continued so all day. The Captain sent me at 8 A.M. up on the main royal to look for the sail that was in sight yesterday, but she was not to be seen, having run away from her during the night. Sent down main-topgallant lifts and overhauled them, and rove new mizzen-topsail braces. At 6 P.M. squared in yards a little and set fore-topmast, -topgallant and main-topgallant studding sails. Speed 6 knots. Course W by S ½ S.

Wednesday, December 6.

During the morning set fore lower studding sail. Wind S and E. Course W by S ½ S. Speed 5 knots. Lat. 20°51′ S.

Thursday, December 7.

At 4 A.M. took in fore lower studding sail. Rove new fore- and main-topgallant runners during the morning. I had a narrow escape today, for the carpenter dropped a heavy hammer from the main-topmast head, which, striking the rim of the top and then glancing off from the bitts forward of the mast, struck me in the shoulder, inflicting rather a harder blow than I was prepared for. Had I been standing up (for I was stooping), I should have got the full force of the blow instead of the bitts. "Many a slip, etc.," and I think it is preferable to have a lame shoulder than a broken head. Course W by S ½ S. Speed 7 knots. Lat. 21°41′ S. Mrs. Hall having sent me several numbers of *Punch*, I had something worth reading all day; she is very kind, having several times before sent me the *Illustrated News*.

**Friday, December 8.**

A beautiful day. Channy's birthday (Mrs. Hall's little son), he being three years old, and of course celebrated in style aft. A large turkey which was brought from Shanghai for the occasion was killed, and quantities of cake, etc., cooked. We forward had apple sauce!! for our duff instead of molasses, in honor of the occasion I suppose. Good luck to Chandler Prince Hall. Poor Jim is, in spite of all that has been done, evidently near his end. I packed his things for him, to be sent home, during the afternoon. God's will be done—he is the only friend I have had since I left home, and there is no sacrifice that I would not make to save him. Set up bobstays and bowsprit shrouds.

**Saturday, December 9.**

Jim passed an easier night than was expected. This morning he was apparently sinking fast, but about 11 A.M. he seemed to rally, being free from pain. The Captain said he was afraid that it was only a bad sign, for all that he had seen die of dysentery, just before death rallied for a while. Wind hauling aft, squared yards and set studding sails, both sides. Set up fore-topmast stay during the morning. Had dried peaches for dinner, an arrangement which is to continue, I hear, for the rest of the voyage. Towards night brailed up spencers.

**Sunday, December 10.**

During the morning sent up both main-royal-studding-sail booms and set the sails, also set main-topmast studding sails, both sides. We have now eleven studding sails set besides our ordinary sail and are literally covered with a cloud of canvas. At 10 A.M. a sail was discovered ahead, about a point off our port bow. Lat. 24°14′ S. Long. 61°27′ E. At 7 P.M. squally; took in all studding sails except port fore-topmast studding sail. During the night set main-topgallant and -royal (both sides), fore lower and -topgallant (port) studding sails. Course W by S. Wind E. A heavy swell set in from E.

**Monday, December 11.**

Rove new port spanker-boom topping lift and set up temporary main-topmast stay. At daylight the sail we saw yesterday was out of sight from the deck, but could be seen from aloft almost out of sight on port beam. Lat. 25°8′ S. At 3 P.M. the main-topgallant sail split from head to foot; unbent it and bent a new sail in its place. Lat. 25°8′ S. Long. 58 E.

Tuesday, December 12.

Jim, since Saturday, has been gradually getting better and, if careful in his diet, will, I think, soon get well. A 6 A.M. set starboard fore lower and -topmast studding sails and braced the yards, the wind being off starboard quarter. At 7 A.M. took in port fore-topgallant studding sail and set it on starboard side. Busy overhauling starboard ratlines. Towards night the wind shifted to NNW; hauled down all studding sails and braced up sharp on starboard tack, heading W and W by S. Lat. 26°3′ S. Long. 56°53′ E.

Wednesday, December 13.

At daylight a sail was discovered ahead, a point off our weather bow; kept overhauling her till 12 P.M., when she was abeam; exchanged signals with her, after which she gradually dropped astern. She was a large Prussian bark under full sail. Saw this morning a large sperm whale about a mile to windward of us, "blowing" in grand style. This is the first whale I ever saw, for tho' "There she blows" has been sung out again and again, somehow or other I never have been lucky enough to see one. At 9 A.M. set spencers. Towards night the wind came out ahead, light and baffling; steering full and by. Lat. 27°16′ S. Brailed up spencers during the night.

Thursday, December 14.

At 12:30 A.M. braced round sharp on port tack, wind light and baffling. My twentieth birthday. At noon it was a dead calm, the sea being only agitated by a heavy swell. The water was filled with "brit," or whales' food; also quantities of bonitos and Portuguese men-of-war were seen about the ship. Busy all day fishing the main yard. At 6 P.M. a breeze sprung up from the S; braced up on port tack, steering W by N and W. During the night set fore lower, -topmast and -topgallant and main-topgallant studding sails, also spencers.

Friday, December 15.

A rainy day. The wind increasing, at 12 M. furled royals and took in studding sails, going 12 knots!! This has been a cheerless day to me; the roof of our room leaking and flooding the floor, and Jim's increased uneasiness and peevishness, keeping me feeling far from cheerful. Today is poor Frank's birthday. Lat. 28°1′ S. At 3 P.M. set main-royal, fore-topmast and main-topgallant studding sails. Course W by N.

Saturday, December 16.

At 7:30 A.M. furled main royal and took in topgallant studding sail. For the first time I was balked in getting on a royal yard, for when I got up, George P. and Harry were one each side of the bunt and, as neither would move, of course I could not climb over them to lay out on the yardarm; the ship plunging and rolling at a tremendous rate made it too dangerous. So I was obliged to lay down, and of course the officers thought I was afraid. Heaven knows I have never yet been afraid to do my duty aloft and that I would have gone on that yard if I had had anything to get hold of fit to trust one's life to. At 9 A.M. took in fore-topmast studding sail. The day before yesterday (Thursday) we were drifting at the rate of 3 knots per hour with the current that sets thro' Mozambique Channel, between Madagascar and the main continent of Africa, in a SW direction. Wind S. Course W. Speed 11 knots. During the afternoon rove new forebraces. By George! it does one's heart good to be flying homeward at the rate we are going. Lat. 29°12′ S. Long. 45°23′ E. At 7 P.M. set fore- and mizzen royals.

Sunday, December 17.

During the morning the wind shifted aft; squared yards and set main-topmast, -topgallant and -royal studding sails (both sides) and fore lower and -topmast studding sails (port). At 12 M. took in royal studding sails. At 4 A.M. furled mizzen-topgallant sail and royal. At 7 A.M. a sail was in sight off our port beam, bound in the opposite direction. During the night the wind shifted off starboard quarter; braced yards and hauled down lee studding sails. Long. 41°16′ E. At 12 midnight set mizzen-topgallant sail.

Monday, December 18.

Wind fresh and squally, at 2 A.M. took in weather studding sails. At 4 A.M. set starboard fore-topmast studding sail. At 7 A.M. set mizzen royal and starboard fore- and main-topgallant studding sails. A large ship was in sight at noon ahead of us, standing the same way, which we gradually passed ahead of, leaving her astern about sunset. Lat. 31°23′ S. Wind NE. Course W by N. At 4 P.M. set starboard fore lower studding sail. Set up main-topgallant and -royal backstays (both sides) during the day. At 11 P.M., looking bad to windward, furled royals and took in all studding sails. The wind began to haul to the S and W.

Tuesday, December 19.

The wind suddenly coming up very strong from S and W, at 2 A.M. called all hands to shorten sail; furled course, close-reefed fore- and main topsails and furled fore- and mizzen topsails. Before we could get the topgallant sails clewed up properly, the wind increased so, that they all three blew into shreds. After reefing, laid aloft again and tried to furl what was left of them; succeeded in furling fore and mizzen and weather yardarm of main; but were obliged to cut away the lee side, the sail slatting about so that it was impossible to lay out on the yard. At 5:30 A.M. set main spencer and hove to under fore-topmast staysail, close-reefed main topsail and spencer; blowing great guns and raining hard all the time we were shortening sail, "Grog ho!" was welcomed by all, after which the watch went below. Wind SSW. Course NW. At 7:30 unrove studding-sail gear, fore and aft. At 8 A.M. close-reefed mizzen topsail and set it; also close-reefed fore-topsail. At 9 A.M. sent down mizzen-topgallant sail and set foresail. 1 P.M. sent down royal-studding-sail booms.

Wednesday, December 20.

Wind moderated. At 4:30 A.M. set reefed spanker and shook reef out of main topsail. At 5 A.M. shook two reefs out of fore-topsail and set mainsail. At 6 A.M. shook reef out of main and mizzen topsails. At 7 A.M. bent a new main-topgallant sail and set it. At 8 A.M. shook remaining reefs out of fore, main, and mizzen topsails and spanker, and set jibs. Wind moderate, going about 5 knots on a NW, NW by N course. A sail was in sight a point abaft the port beam from main-topgallant yard at 7 A.M. At 9 A.M. bent a new fore-topgallant sail; set it, also fore- and main royals, and braced up sharp, steering full and by W ½ N. Lat. 31° S. At noon quantities of dolphin were playing around the ship, chasing flying fish. At 4 P.M. bent mizzen-topgallant sail (which both watches have been busy repairing, there being no spare mizzen-topgallant sail in the ship) and set it, also mizzen royal.

Thursday, December 21.

4 A.M. wind N and W. Steering W, braced on starboard tack. At noon, wind hauled aft; squared in yards and set fore lower and -top-mast and main-topgallant studding sails, both sides. During the day spliced port main-topgallant breast backstay, which had stranded; also sent down new topmast-studding-sail booms. At 11:30 P.M., heavy squalls off lee bow working around ahead to windward, took in all studding sails and furled royals. Lat. 31°9′ S.

Friday, December 22.

At 1 A.M. clewed up topgallant sails. At daylight, clearing off, set topgallant sails, at 7 A.M. main royal and at 8 fore- and mizzen royals. Wind off starboard quarter, set starboard main-topgallant and fore lower, -topmast and -topgallant studding sails. At 11 P.M. took in studding sails and furled royals, the lower studding sail and fore-royal having blown to shreds. Wind NE. Course W by S.

Saturday, December 23.

At 7 A.M. set main royal. During the morning sent down fore-royal, got a new one up and bent it; Charley Bates hauling out one earing and I, the other, furled it. Set studding sails, but at noon, a heavy black cloud passing astern and the wind variable, furled main royal, hauled up mainsail, clewed up topgallant sails and hauled down studding sails. At 3 P.M., the haze lifting, a large ship was in sight off our starboard beam, standing same course. The weather brightening up, set topgallant sails, main royal and jibs. Wind fresh and squally, at 5 furled main royal; at 7, fore- and mizzen-topgallant sails. Blowing hard and looking very black to windward, and thundering heavily accompanied by most vivid chain lightning, at 10 P.M. called all hands, furled main-topgallant sail, jibs and mainsail, hauled up foresail and double-reeefed topsails. At 11:30 P.M. the ship that was in sight during the afternoon passed within ¼ mile off our lee quarter, showed her light and was soon out of sight ahead, standing on under topgallant sails. A heavy sea all day from N and W.

Sunday, December 24.

During the morning, cloudy, blowing fresh, shook a reef out of top-sails, set mainsail, foresail, jibs, fore- and main-topgallant sails; heading W by S. Thro' the haze, 3 points off our weather bow at 7 A.M. saw a sail supposed to be the one that passed us during the night on port tack. At 11 A.M. called all hands and went about on port tack, heading NW by WNW. While going about, the fore-bowline not being let go, the starboard leech of the foresail ripped from head to foot; unbent it, got out a new sail and bent it. At 1:30 P.M. squally, blowing hard in puffs, called all hands, close-reefed fore- and mizzen topsails and double-reefed main topsail, furled jibs and mainsail, hauled up foresail and set reefed spanker and spencers. Heavy sea from N and W. At noon sail out of sight. For the last day or so Cape pigeons and two or three albatross have been hovering round the ship. The weather is right cold, and the sky wears that gloomy aspect only to be met with off the Horn. 8 P.M. Christmas Eve. What a different Eve this is from the last. A year ago today I was at work on board the *Great Republic*, and now I am off the Cape of Good Hope under short sail, pitching about at a great rate. A happy night this is at home. Hen and Moll, the ducks, are nodding their wise heads over the surprises of the morrow, while perchance a thought of me arises in the minds of all. My presents are in my chest, such as they are; for as ill luck had it, while in Hong Kong I bought nothing, tho' I had splendid chances, trusting to better luck in Shanghai, where I found too late that there was nothing worth buying.

Monday, December 25.

Merry Christmas. When our watch came on deck at midnight, every star shone as bright as could be and the Southern Cross and Magellan's Clouds were in plain sight. The wind had moderated, and we began to make sail at 8 A.M., having shook all reefs out and set topgallant sails and royals. At 8 unbent outer jib, which had split, and bent a new one, after which we set jibs. Land 70 miles distant. Course WNW. Wind S and W. At noon squared in yards a little and set port fore-topmast and -topgallant and main-topgallant studding sails. At 3 P.M. a sail was discovered off our lee bow ahead, being in all probability the ship that passed us on Saturday night and which was seen also yesterday for a while, passing out of sight on opposite tack. Lat. 35°13′ S. This is the second Christmas that I have passed at work, and many more will be spent the same way, I am afraid. At 8 P.M. furled fore-royal, the wind being dead aft. At 11 P.M. set port fore lower studding sail and hauled down jibs.

Tuesday, December 26.

A beautiful day. The wind shifting off starboard quarter (E by S, ESE), braced yards at 4 A.M. and shifted all lee studding sails to windward. At 7 A.M. set fore-royal. While loosing the royal I looked all around to see if I could see the sail, but she was "non inventus," having run away from us during the night, being the first craft this voyage that has beat us. At 8 A.M. set jibs. At noon, wind E, steering NW ½ W. At 5 P.M. a sail was discovered 3 points off weather (port) bow, the wind shifting to port quarter at 3 P.M. The Captain said we would probably pass Cape Agulhas at midnight.

Wednesday, December 27.

A beautiful day. Wind dead aft, studding sails set both sides. At 5 A.M. altered ship's course, heading NNW. Passed Agulhas during last night. At noon we were in Lat. 34°54′ S, the Cape being about 30 miles to the N of us. Busy overhauling main brace pendants. I was a great part of the morning below taking an inventory of ship's sheets, towels, etc. Mrs. Hall sent Jim a bottle of Malaga wine to drink; very kind in her. At 1:40 P.M. passed the meridian of the Cape and are now once more in the Atlantic. The sail we saw yesterday was not in sight at daylight, having probably dropped astern during the night. Saw a Mother Carey's chicken this afternoon, the first I have seen in a long while. During the afternoon, wind shifted off port quarter; braced yards and hauled down lee studding sails. At 5 P.M. set spencers. Wind S and W. Speed 10 knots. At 11 P.M. cloudy, wind freshening, furled fore-royal, clewed up main and mizzen royals, and took in all studding sails. Wind hauling ahead, braced yards.

## Thursday, December 28.

At daylight set royals. Wind SW. Course NNW. Busy stoppering starboard after main-topmast backstay, which had rotted under the service in the wake of the main yard, and sewing the backstays on the other side in the same place. At 11 P.M. squared yards a little and set fore lower, -topmast and -topgallant and main-topgallant studding sails.

## Friday, December 29.

During the morning sent down mizzen-topmast stay, overhauled it and sent it up again. At noon squared in yards a little. Course NW by N. Wind S and W. A heavy swell from S and W set in during the afternoon. At 5 P.M. unbent the new foresail and bent the old one, which had been mended, in its place.

## Saturday, December 30.

At 5 A.M. a sail was discovered ahead, a point off starboard bow. At 7 A.M., wind dead aft, squared yards and set studding sails, both sides, and then began to overhaul the sail fast. At 10 A.M. made her out to be a full-rigged ship under a cloud of canvas (main skysail, royal studding sails, etc.). As soon as the Captain saw the royal studding sails, he gave order to have ours set, so the booms were sent up and the studding sails set, both sides. And now the race was exciting. At 2 P.M. the wind hauled on port quarter; braced yards and hauled down lee fore studding sails. We now began to gain fast, for the wind was increasing and enabled us to set staysails and jibs. At 2:30 she began to yaw, back and forth, evidently with the intention of speaking to us. At 3 she was within hailing distance and proved to be the *Ariel*, Captain Ayres, which sailed ten days before us, and of which Jim Allen went 1st mate. Captain Ayres said that he was in company with the *Messenger* off the Cape and that the *Panama* was sixteen days to Sunda. We then exchanged longitudes, ours 8°21′, his 8°23′ E, after which we passed ahead of her. From the *Ariel*'s being in company with the *Messenger* so lately, we have some slight hopes of measuring speed with her, yet. It was the noblest sight I ever saw, to see the *Ariel*, one mass of canvas (having thirty-two sails set), rising and sinking in the swell like a thing of life. A bright moonlight night. At midnight the *Ariel* could be seen, when the moon shone fair on her sails, about a mile astern. Hauled down lee main studding sails.

Sunday, December 31.

The last day of the old year. At daylight the *Ariel*'s topsails could just be seen above the horizon, and at noon she was out of sight. All night long we had a crashing breeze going 11 and 12 knots per hour. Wind S and W, yards squared in. Course NW by N ½ N. Lat. 28°36′ S. Long. 5° E.

Monday, January 1, 1855.

Happy New Year. A few rain clouds ushered in the day, but as the sun rose they soon passed away and we had a most lovely day, a 10-knot breeze sending us on our way rejoicing. The old year was seen out and the New Year in by both watches of boys in a most original way. Christmas, our watch formed the Brass Heads, a society for mutual fun, meeting around the capstan every other night, where we discuss the gossip of the day and relate any amusing incident that has come to notice. The other watch formed the Snatch Block Guard, so named because their domine the 3d mate—alias Theodosius Snatch Block— rarely opens his mouth unless to say, "One of you boys get a snatch block." At midnight, the S.B.s had a procession round the ship, carrying their namesake aloft and repeating an extempore poem which, tho' not written by Shakespeare, still answered for the occasion. "O ye S.Bs look ferocious, Were the last dying words of Theodosius," after which Somnus engaged their attention the remainder of the watch. For my part the new year was ushered in by a swinging toothache. During the day the SE trades set in; squared yards, clewed up after sails, furling topgallant sails and royals and setting studding sails alow and aloft.

Tuesday, January 2.

At 9 A.M. sent main-topmast-studding-sail booms up and set the sails. Busy scraping ironwork preparatory to painting, and rattling down mizzen-lower and mizzen-topmast rigging. Lat. 24°54′ S. Long. 1°3′ W. Course NW by N. Speed 9 knots. At 1 P.M. unbent the cross-jack in order to repair it.

Wednesday, January 3.

At 7 A.M. set after sails, which, however, were clewed up again at 10, wind aft. Busy rattling down and painting ironwork. Wind SE. Course NW by N ½ N. Mrs. Hall gave Jim another bottle of wine and told him whenever he got out of it to come to her and she would give him more. She is a lady every inch, and I never shall forget her kindness to Jim. She keeps me and him supplied with books, sending Channy to our room almost every week; very kind. At 6 P.M. bent crossjack and furled mizzen-topgallant sail and royal.

Thursday, January 4.

This morning I was subjected to one of a series of mean petty spite vented on me by Mr. Lind (I suppose because he never has had his due amount of respect showed him and because I insulted him in Shanghai one afternoon when he had charge of the deck, by doubting his word, and had some high words with him about it), for he broke up my hen coop. He also killed one of Bob's fowl, a noble Shanghai, by his brutally knocking it around while in the coop, ostensibly wash-ing the coop out! ! At 10 A.M. unbent mizzen topsail and spread it on poop to mend it. Wind SE. Course NW by N. Lat. 21°45′ S.

Friday, January 5.

During the night someone tarred Lind's monkey, and great was the row that was raised. The mate said that as the tarring had begun he would give us a chance to finish, so he got the tar out and set Star watch, who did it, at work, till he found out the guilty one, for at noon Ned and George L. owned up. When our watch came on deck he allowed the rest of their watch to go below but kept them at it all day, a sufficient dose to pay for ill-timed sport. We nearly finished the mizzen, a good day's work. Course NW by N ½ N. Wind E.

Saturday, January 6.

Took all mats off main and fore swifters and -stays in order to tar. Bent mizzen topsail and set it, also topgallant sail and royal. Wind shifting to N and E at noon, braced yards on starboard tack and hauled down lee studding sails, also weather lower studding sail. Course NW. Tarred mizzen rigging in the afternoon. Lat. 18°9′ S.

Sunday, January 7.

At 4 A.M., the wind S and E, squared yards and set lee main studding sails. Lat. 17°25′ S. Course NW by N. Wind light.

Monday, January 8.

Tarred main, all except lower rigging. Lat. 15°49′ S. Long. 15°30′ W. Wind S and E till sunset, when it shifted to N and E; braced yards, took in lee studding sails. At 11 P.M. set main spencer.

Tuesday, January 9.

Nearly finished tarring on fore, except topmast and lower rigging; a couple of days work will finish tarring down. Lat. 14°20′ S (9 A.M.). Long. 18°24′30″ W. Chronometer loses 2″.

Wednesday, January 10.

At daylight the main-topmast studding sail split; bent a new one. During the day, overhauled and set up lee jib guys; also busy tarring lower riggings and lanyards. Wind E by N. Course NNW. Lat. 12°20′ S (9 A.M.). Long. 20°33′ W.

Thursday, January 11.

Scrubbed paintwork and painted poop during the morning. Bent main-topgallant staysail at noon. Boys busy tarring lanyards. Course NW by N. Lat. 9°57′ S. Long. 23°49′30″ W (2:30 P.M.).

Friday, January 12.

Busy preparing for port; scrubbed and painted port rail, planed and varnished spare booms, and overhauled and set up weather jib guys.

At 5 P.M. a large clipper was in sight, standing S and W, close-hauled, an outward-bounder. Wind S and E. Course NNE, NW by N. Lat. 8° 12′ S. Long. 25° 50′ 45″ W (9 A.M.).

Saturday, January 13.

At daylight another outward-bound sail was in sight. Lat. 4° 56′ S. Long. 29° 48′ W (2 P.M.). Wind ESE. Course NNW, NW by W. Busy scrubbing and painting; painted top of house, starboard rails and break of forecastle.

Sunday, January 14.

A beautiful day. Wind SE. Course NNW. Lat. 2° 8′ S. Long. 31° 43′ 30″ W (3 P.M.). With luck we'll soon be home, in three weeks, most glorious to think of!

Monday, January 15.

Crossed the Line about 5 A.M. in Long. 32° 50′ W. During the morning scrubbed and painted house. In the afternoon began to scrape chain plates. Lat. 1° 4′ N. Long. 33° 57′ 30″ W (3 P.M.). During the night the wind began to haul aft; squared in yards till Ben and 3d mate had a fight about the water.

Tuesday, January 16.

At 10 A.M., yards square, hoisted port main and fore studding sails. The wind seems to be unsettled, first off one quarter and then off the other. Course NW by N. Wind SE. Lat. 3° 20′ N. Long. 36° 24′ W (2 P.M.).

Wednesday, January 17.

Busy preparing for port, painting lower masts, etc. Towards night, wind off starboard quarter, hauled down lee studding sails and braced yards. At 10 P.M. a squall struck us; came near getting aback. Lat. 5° 20′ N. Long. 38° 33′ W (2:30 P.M.). The night was beautiful and the Dipper was in plain sight, having been so for several days.

Thursday, January 18.

Painted waterways, spare topmasts, etc. Towards night the wind began to die away. At 10 P.M. squally, took in all studding sails, wind off port quarter. Lat. 7°44′ N. Long. 40°17′ W (3 P.M.).

Friday, January 19.

Almost becalmed. At 10 A.M. wind came in squally from N and E, braced yards and all thought the trades had begun, but by 11 the wind had died away and left us almost totally becalmed again, averaging about 1 knot. Lat. 8°48′ N. Long. 41°54′ W (2:30 P.M.).

Saturday, January 20.

Squally. At 12 M. furled royals and mizzen-topgallant sail and clewed up fore and main. Unrove port studding-sail gear and sent down royal-studding-sail booms. At 2 P.M. made sail again. The wind was squally all day, from ENE, NE. At 6 P.M. furled fore- and mizzen royals. Course NW. Lat. 10°8′ N. Long. 43°56′ W (2:30 P.M.).

Sunday, January 21.

At 7 A.M., wind hauling aft, squared in yards and set starboard fore studding sails and main-topgallant studding sail and royals. Squally all day. Towards night took in studding sails and at 8 P.M. furled royals. Heavy squalls. At 10 P.M. furled topgallant sails and stood by topsail halyards. Course NW. Lat. 11°10′ N. Long. 45°44′ W (2 P.M.).

Monday, January 22.

A heavy squall at 4 A.M. The wind towards morning hauled aft and was steadier; set topgallant sails, royals, staysails and main spencer, also fore studding sails and main-topgallant studding sail. At noon, wind hauling ahead, braced yards and hauled down topgallant studding sails. Busy pounding rust off of and painting anchors and scraping tar pots. At 7 P.M. squally; hauled down topmast studding sail and clewed up royals. At 10 P.M. almost a dead calm. Lat. 13°24′ N. Long 48°5′ W (9:30 A.M.).

Tuesday, January 23.

At 7 A.M. rainy; a strong breeze sprang up from NE. Braced yards up sharp and set royals. At 8 cleared off, and the wind for the remainder of the day was light. Got up a Manila hawser and made preventer main-topmast backstays during the day. Lat. 14°18′ N. Long. 50°36′ W (2:30 P.M.).

Wednesday, January 24.

Strong breezes. At 7 A.M. set topgallant and fore-topmast studding sails. Heavy squalls passing over us; clewed up royals three times during the morning and took in studding sails. The old ship seems to smell New York now, for she is averaging 10 knots and has been nearly all day. Busy scrubbing and painting sides. Course NW, NW by N. Wind ENE. Lat. 15°47′ N. Long. 52°21′ W (9 A.M.).

Thursday, January 25.

At 8 A.M., wind aft, set fore studding sails and main-topgallant studding sail. A sperm whale was in plain sight to leeward during the afternoon. All hands busy scrubbing and painting sides. At 4 P.M. bent new fore-topsail. Quantities of gulfweed were floating by all day long. Towards night the wind began to die away and we were only averaging 4 or 5 knots. Lat. 18°47′ N. Long. 55°32′ W (2 P.M.).

Friday, January 26.

At 6 A.M., wind SE, set port fore-topmast and main-topgallant studding sails and hauled down outer jib and staysails and brailed up main spencer. At 6 P.M. hauled down port fore-topmast studding sail and braced yards a little; set jib and staysails. Had an addition to our stock during the evening in the shape of two lambs. Wind S and E. Lat. 19°46′ N. Long. 56°46′ W (2 P.M.).

Saturday, January 27.

Mrs. Hall's youngest child, George C., died this morning and was put into a small cask of rum during the forenoon watch in order to preserve it for burial ashore. Yesterday morn he was perfectly well, but at noon was taken with croup, which proved fatal. A most beautiful day, flying fish and dolphins playing around the bows. At 10 A.M. the 2d and 3d mates had a fight, which ended in Mr. Cornell getting the worst of it when the Captain separated them. Fun in the higher circles! ! In the afternoon bent new foresail. Wind S and E. Course NW. Lat. 20°58′ N. Long. 58°9′ W (2:30 P.M.). At noon set topmast (main) studding sails and port fore lower and -topmast studding sails. Our steward Mattison was with Father in the *Raritan* and Uncle Lynch in the Dead Sea expedition, so he has told me several times since we sailed from Shanghai, and has sailed with Frank in the *Boston* and the *Savannah*. At 6 P.M. hauled down port studding sails.

Sunday, January 28.

A most lovely day. Quantities of gulfweed floating by, I managed to get some; put some in a bottle to take home. In one piece I found a little crab about as big as my thumbnail, a lively little customer, for he got overboard before I could secure him. At 9 A.M. a sail was discovered off weather bow. Several rain showers passed over us during the day, each of which was succeeded by a splendid rainbow. Lat. 22°17′ N. Long. 59°35′ W (9:30 A.M.).

Monday, January 29.

At daylight the sail discovered yesterday was astern off our weather quarter. During the day bent new jib and main topsail, the latter a brand new sail, never having been bent before. At 3 P.M. passed a large schooner standing to S and W. Saw Mother Carey's chickens about the ship for the first time since leaving the Cape. Lat. 24°20′ N. Long. 62°40′ W (3 P.M.).

Tuesday, January 30.

In the evening, wind aft, set port studding sails. Scraped royal masts and spare topgallant masts. We were surrounded by gulfweed all day, large fields of it floating by continually. Lat. 25°54′ N. Long. 64°23′ W (9 A.M.). 1,130 miles from New York.

Wednesday, January 31.

A lovely day. The sky looked rather wintry, but still it was warm enough for thin clothes. The wind hauled off port quarter during the morning, S. At noon bent new mainsail. At 1 P.M. passed a brig off port beam standing N. Lat. 27°32′ N. Long. 66°29′ W (3 P.M.). Wind increasing, at 11:30 P.M. hauled down topgallant studding sails and furled royals.

Thursday, February 1.

Wind hauling to the W. At 12:30 A.M. exchanged signals with a schooner standing S. At 3 A.M. furled outer jib and hauled down studding sails. Wind increasing, at 3:30 furled crossjack and mizzen-topgallant sail. At 4 A.M. called all hands, furled mainsail and inner jib, hauled up foresail and double-reefed topsails. Wind and sea increasing, wind N and W, furled fore- and mizzen topsails and close-reefed main topsail; hove to under closs-reefed main topsail, main spencer and fore-topmast staysail. It was hard work shortening sail; cold as ice and raining hard made it difficult work handling the sails, they were so stiff. Towards daylight it began to thunder and lighten, which continued for about an hour at short intervals. While reefing main topsail the main-topgallant-studding-sail boom got loose; had to send it down. During the morning unrove studding-sail gear, fore and aft. At 10 A.M. furled foresail, wind NW. Lat. 30°8′ N (12 noon). At 2 P.M. set close-reefed fore-topsail and at 3 close-reefed mizzen top-sail. At 4 P.M. exchanged signals with a hermaphrodite brig outward-bound. At 4:30 set reefed foresail. 8 P.M. set inner jib and reefed spanker. At 12 M. shook reef out of foresail and set reefed mainsail.

Friday, February 2.

At 4 A.M. shook reef out of mainsail. During the morning watch sent down main-topgallant sail to mend, having been torn while furling. At 8 A.M., heading NE, wore ship, standing WSW-W on starboard tack. At 9 A.M. shook reefs out of main and mizzen topsails and two out of fore-topsail and set outer jib, wind and sea having gone down. At 9:30 bent main-topgallant sail and set it, together with fore- and mizzen-topgallant sails. At noon, calm with a heavy swell. In the afternoon sent down royal yards and two staysails. All the afternoon it looked and felt as if it was going to snow. 4 P.M., going about ½ knot, braced yards round on port tack. Lat. 30°45′ N. Long. 67°30′ W (2:30 P.M.). Sent down main-topmast-studding-sail booms in the

morning and studding-sail halyard blocks, fore and aft, in the afternoon; also took both quarter boats inboard. At 5 P.M. squared in
yards, steering NW, light breeze SW. Here we are, within forty-eight
hours sail of home, and hardly any wind! Discouraging, I declare. At
7 P.M. wind came out strong from SW.

Saturday, February 3.

Wind increasing, at 3 A.M. furled topgallant sails. At 4 A.M. called
all hands to shorten sail, blowing hard and rain falling in torrents;
double-reefed fore- and main topsails, clewed up former, reefed mainsail, hauled up foresail and furled jibs, after which the watch went
below. At 6 A.M. (heavy sea) called all hands, furled mainsail, close-
reefed main topsail, clewed up mizzen topsail and hove to under main
spencer, close-reefed main topsail and fore-topmast staysail. Wind
NW, cold as ice. 7 A.M. a sail was discovered ahead, a large ship under
close-reefed topsails, standing S, an outward-bounder. At 7:30 it
cleared off and made sail; set reefed mainsail and foresail, single-
reefed mizzen topsail, double-reefed fore-topsail and outer jib. 8 A.M.
wore ship, standing on port tack. 9 A.M. shook reef out of mainsail.
10 A.M. wore ship, standing NNW, wind W. At 10:30 shook a reef out
of main topsail. 11:30 shook a reef out of fore- and main topsails and
set fore- and main-topgallant sails. Lat. 31°54′ N. Long. 68°58′ W (2:30
P.M.). 2 P.M. a ship in sight to starboard, standing S. 4 P.M. furled fore-
topgallant sail and, soon after, main-topgallant sail. 4:30 P.M. another
outward-bounder in sight off port beam, a large ship under double-
reefed topsails and reefed foresail and mainsail. 6 P.M. heavy sea and
blowing harder; called all hands, double-reefed fore- and main topsails and furled spanker and mainsail. At 8 P.M. close-reefed mizzen
topsail. At 12 P.M. called all hands, close-reefed fore-topsail and reefed
foresail. Saw several "corpusans"* during the night.

Sunday, February 4.

At 4 A.M. all hands again; close-reefed main topsail. Last night was
the worst night that I have seen at sea. Tho' clear, the wind was awful
cold and the sea very heavy; and we pitched, literally speaking, thro'
the night, shipping water every little while. Steering N. At 6 A.M.

* Corposant, or Saint Elmo's fire—*Ed.*

(daylight) set mainsail (reefed). 6 P.M. furled mainsail. Wind SW. Course NW by W, NW, NW by N. At 9 P.M. set reefed mainsail, reefed spanker and jib. 10 P.M. shook reef out of fore- and main topsails and foresail. Towards midnight, wind and sea increased.

Monday, February 5.

At 3 A.M. blowing a gale; called all hands, close-reefed fore- and main topsails and foresail. At 5 furled mainsail. At 6 all hands again, blowing a living gale; furled fore- and main topsails. This is the worst gale we have had since we left New York, and the first time we have been obliged to furl the main topsail. The sea is the heaviest I ever saw, running almost mountain high, so to speak, and breaking over us every little while, keeping us continually wet, fore and aft. Wind SW. Steering NW by W. At 8 A.M. a large bark passed across our bows about a mile distant, standing to the E, under single-reefed main topsail, double-reefed fore-topsail, reefed foresail and fore-topmast staysail, mizzen-topmast and fore-topgallant mast struck. At 3 P.M. almost as black as night and wind and sea increasing; called all hands and furled foresail, hove to under main spencer and fore-topmast staysail. While aloft it began to thunder and lighten, and rain fell in torrents. While getting "grog" a bolt of lightning broke over the ship between the mainmast and mizzen mast with a report like a large cannon. For a few minutes all was confusion, the shock knocking the mate and nearly all hands down. For my part the effect on me was precisely as if a heavy electric battery had discharged its full force on my system, racking every nerve from my shoulder down and leaving my back as sore as if it had been struck a heavy blow and very weak for sometime after. When it struck me, it doubled me up just like a ball; and there I hung to a bight, hardly knowing anything for a second or so, when it flashed across my mind that the lightning had told fatally on some of the crew and that perhaps it would paralyze one of my legs or both. I never suffered so much in mind in so short a time in my whole life before. Mr. Larrabee told Burt afterwards that he might go to sea all his life and never see such a terrific gale again as the one today. Lat. 35°9′ N (12 noon). At 5 P.M. the wind began to go down; called all hands and set foresail (reefed). At 7 P.M. the wind began to haul ahead and at 10 P.M. came out strong from NW by N, accompanied by rain and sleet; braced round yards on starboard tack.

Tuesday, February 6.

At 2 A.M. set close-reefed main topsail, heading WSW. Towards morning, wind hauled to N. At 7:30 A.M. set close-reefed spanker, steering due W. Last night was a hard night, raining hard and squally, one squall carrying away main-spencer vang and gaff and spanker sheets, giving us work for a watch to repair the damage. At 9 A.M. water 66°, wind 56°. 10 A.M. set close-reefed fore-topsail. At noon a large bark outward- bound passed us, under foresail, reefed mainsail, double-reefed fore- and single-reefed main topsails, mizzen- and fore-topmast staysails, and reefed jib. At 3 P.M. heavy squalls; called all hands and furled fore-topsail. Saw a great many gulls flying round the ship.

Wednesday, February 7.

Towards 12 P.M. the wind going down; between 12 and 4 A.M. set close-reefed fore- and mizzen topsails, whole mainsail, and jib, and shook reef out of foresail. From 4 to 8 A.M. shook two reefs out of topsails. At 3 A.M. wind began to shift and at 6 A.M., coming out SW, wore ship, heading NW. At 9 A.M. set fore- and main- and at 9:30 mizzen-topgallant sails and shook close reef out of spanker. At noon going 9 knots! ! Clear and cold. During the afternoon sent down fore-topmast-studding-sail booms. At 1:30 P.M., going 12 knots, furled top-gallant sails. Wind increasing; at 2, single-reefed mizzen topsail. At 3:30, called all hands and double-reefed topsails. At 4, close-reefed mizzen topsail. At 6 P.M., called all hands and reefed courses. At 8, called all hands, furled mainsail, closereefed fore- and main topsails and furled the former. "Grog ho!" was a welcome sound. At 10 P.M. furled mizzen topsail. All night we were averaging 8 knots on a NW course, wind well aft.

Thursday, February 8.

Squally till daylight. At 2 A.M. set close-reefed fore-topsail and at 3 called all hands to furl it. At 5, the wind headed us off to a NE by E course, blowing hard and rain falling in torrents till 7 A.M., when it lulled; called all hands and wore ship. We were in the Gulf Stream all night, tho' when we entered it I could not find out; at 6 A.M. air 62°, water 74°; lightning all night at intervals, another indication of the stream. I wish we could get in, for this calling all hands two or three times a night is hard work. During the morning, wind N and E, steering NNW, set jib, close-reefed fore- and mizzen topsails. At 3 P.M. wind heading us off and squally; furled mizzen topsail and jib and set close-reefed spanker. Lat. 36°45′ N. Long. 72°49′ W (8:30 A.M.). At 7:30 all hands again and furled fore-topsail. 8 P.M. wore ship, steering NE on port tack. At 10 P.M. exchanged signals, i.e., showed light, with an outward-bound ship.

### Friday, February 9.

At 1:30 A.M. wore ship, steering W by N on starboard tack. 2:30 set close-reefed mizzen topsail. 4 A.M. set fore-topsail and jib. At 6 set reefed mainsail and shook reef out of foresail and spanker. At daylight, clear as a bell, we were bowling along merrily WSW; three sail ahead, coasting craft. During the morning got up 45 fathoms of each cable. At noon shook a reef out of topsails and mainsail. 1 P.M. two sail ahead off lee bow, schooners inward-bound. During the afternoon passed five more sail, viz: two schooners, a brig, a ship and a bark also bound in. At 4 P.M. called all hands, reefed courses, close-reefed topsails and furled jib. At 6 P.M. all hands again; furled mainsail and wore ship, steering ENE. Cold as ice and sleeting. "Grog ho!" needed no urging to be accepted. At 7 P.M. furled mizzen topsail. Lat. 37°44′ N at noon. 8 P.M. called all hands and furled fore-topsail. 12 midnight all hands again and wore ship, standing W, W by N. Blowing hard all night. We were obliged to keep a most vigilant watch and show lanterns, fore and aft, all night long, as we were surrounded by vessels whose lights we could see at times on all sides.

### Saturday, February 10.

O misery! last night was awful, so cold I thought I should freeze, and sleeting; every rope like a bar of iron. Toward daylight made sail, set close-reefed fore- and mizzen topsails and close-reefed spanker. At 8 A.M. set reefed mainsail. At 8:30 passed two sail, a bark under close-reefed topsails and a brigantine hove to under main staysail. Snow fell several times during the morning, but luckily not in any quantity. During the morning shook reef out of foresail and fore- and main topsails and set jib. At 3 P.M. shook a reef out of mizzen topsail and spanker. Towards night the wind began to die away. At 8 P.M. reefed foresail, furled spanker and jib. Lat. 37°2′ N (12 noon). Wind light, at 11 P.M. set spanker and jib. Heading all night W, W ½ N. At 12 P.M. set mainsail and foresail (whole).

Sunday, February 11.

A lovely day. Between 4 and 8 A.M. shook another reef out of top-sails and set topgallant sails. Going about 5 knots. Three sail in sight, a ship, a brigantine and schooner, which we passed towards noon and soon left astern. After such weather as we have had, such a day as today is a perfect Godsend. Sounded twice during the morning, find-ing no bottom at 80 fathoms. Lat. 37°15′ N (12 noon). Long. 73°51′ W (8 A.M.). Light breezes all day, varying from NE by N to NW. At noon tried to go about but missed stays and kept on same tack. Wind increasing, at 11 P.M. furled mizzen-topgallant sail. At 12 P.M. went about on port tack.

Monday, February 12.

A clear, cold day, the thermometer being 37° at noon. At 2 A.M. furled fore- and main-topgallant sails. At 4 A.M. called all hands and double-reefed fore- and main topsails. At 6 A.M. single-reefed mizzen topsail. During the morning shook a reef out of fore- and main top-sails and set fore- and main-topgallant sails. At 4 P.M. shook a reef out of mizzen topsail and set topgallant sail. Also sounded, getting sandy bottom at 35 fathoms. At noon passed a bark. At 3 P.M. a ship and schooner were in sight off weather bow. At 4 P.M. eleven sail were in sight from aloft, viz: six ahead, two to leeward and three astern. Lat. 37°26′ N (12 noon). Steering NW, NW ½ N all day on starboard tack, having wore ship at 7 A.M. Busy scraping masts and unbending stud-ding sails. Towards night the wind came out from E.

Tuesday, February 13.

At 2 A.M. hove the lead, getting bottom at 15 fathoms; called all hands and went about on port tack, heading ESE. At 3 passed a ship and a brig. Busy all the morning getting up cable; got up 45 fathoms small and 30 large cable, and overhauled range forward of windlass. Passed, during the morning, twelve craft, two of them barks. At 2

P.M. a large propeller passed astern of us, standing W, probably from Boston to Philadelphia. Heading all day NNE, starboard tacks aboard, having gone about at 7 A.M., when we shook remaining reefs out, fore and aft. At sunset several sail in sight. At 5 P.M. called all hands to shorten sail, furled topgallant sails, double-reefed topsails and reefed spanker and mainsail. Tonight, it is to be hoped, is my last night out for this voyage, Sandy Hook being about 50 miles off. At 8 reefed foresail and hauled it and mainsail up. Wind increased to a gale during the night.

Wednesday, February 14.

St. Valentines Day. At 7 A.M. furled the mainsail. At daylight fifteen sail in sight, viz: four inward-bound and one outward-bound ships, the latter a large clipper, three barks, four brigs and three schooners. At 8 A.M. called all hands and got port anchor over the bows. At 8:30 wore ship and stood S; also set foresail. The lightship was in sight at 9 A.M. Here's a fix; instead of going in today, here we are, a cold, foggy, rainy day, no pilot and standing offshore! I believe the Captain is an imbecile, for last night, when he might have made, he shortened sail, and today other craft are standing on under topgallant sails and courses with the jack at the fore, while we are going S. Most think he has forgot a box in Shanghai and is going back after it. At noon, fog very thick, took a pilot and at once wore ship and stood in. At 3 P.M. came near a collision with the *Hudson*, Glasgow packet, she bearing right down on us and discovering us just in time to wear ship. Five minutes longer and a pretty mess we'd have been in. Fog so thick and land only a mile or so distant, the Highland and Sandy Hook lights in sight, close-reefed topsails, reefed courses and stood offshore. The pilot says that all the craft that we saw this morning got in and that it was the Captain's fault we were not in also, and that it was all luck we got a pilot as we were out of pilot ground, and that if his boat had not been the last one down he would not have stood out so far. Humbugging with the braces and courses all night, raining all the time. The Captain and steward both drunk and quarreling all night.

Thursday, February 15.

At daylight made sail, shook reefs out of courses, two reefs out of topsails and main-topgallant sail, wore ship and stood in. At noon the fog lifted for about an hour, when it came on thick as ever again. At 5 P.M. shortened sail, furled mainsail and main-topgallant sail and close-reefed topsails. The pilot gave his opinion pretty freely to the mate about matters being particularly severe on our being so short-handed, saying we ought to have thirty-six instead of twelve men to work a ship like this and that if anything happens we will lose insurance. The Captain under the influence of liquor (intoxicated) all day and quarreling with the steward. Whatever happens to me, God deliver me from a drunken Captain. The men are all well nigh discouraged and curse him openly and loudly. Everything is like iron, ropes stiff and hard, sails wet and almost impossible to handle, and, to add to all, the pilot expects a gale of wind.

Friday, February 16.

Passed the "Narrows."

And so ends my first voyage.


October 26, 1856

Remember, this is a private journal.
H.M.G.

# Data

1854

| | |
|---|---|
| Friday, February 24 | Sailed from New York |
| Sunday, February 26 | Crossed Gulf Stream |
| Sunday, March 19 | 9 A.M. sighted Saint Paul Island, Lat. 0°55′ N, Long. 29°22′ W |
| | 7 P.M. crossed the Line |
| Monday, April 17 | T. Livingston fell overboard at 7 A.M. and was lost |
| Thursday, April 20 | 4:30 P.M. Staten Island in sight |
| Sunday, April 23 | Cape Horn in sight |
| Tuesday, April 25 | 7 A.M. sighted Diego Ramirez, Lat. 56°29′ S Long. 68°43′ W |
| Wednesday, June 21 | 9 A.M. passed Farallon Islands and at 2 P.M. were fast alongside Broadway wharf |
| Sunday, July 2 | "Vide" |
| Monday, July 3 | 6 A.M. took steam and bid adieu to San Francisco |
| | 1 P.M. stood off under all sail |
| Wednesday, July 12 | Sighted Sandwich Islands |
| Saturday, August 12 | Sighted Babuyan Islands, at the entrance to the China seas, extending from Lat. 19°1′ to 19°28′ N, and from Long. 121°10′ to to 122°12′ E |
| Friday, August 18 | Twelve islands in sight |
| Saturday, August 19 | Anchored about 8 miles below Hong Kong |
| Monday, August 21 | Took a steamer at 6 P.M. and at 9:30 dropped anchor about a mile from Victoria Town |
| Thursday, August 31 | 11 A.M. weighed anchor and stood out to sea by Lyeemoon Pass |
| Thursday, September 7 | Island of Formosa in sight |
| Friday, September 8 | 4 P.M. sighted island of Pih-Ki-Shan |
| Monday, September 11 | 5 P.M. sighted the islands of Chu San, Lat. 30°1′ N, Long. 122°6′ E |
| Wednesday, September 13 | Land in sight at daylight, islands—Four Sisters, Two Brothers—Lucona and Barren |

| Thursday, September 14 | 3 P.M. dropped anchor 6 miles from Wuhsien |
| Saturday, September 16 | 6:30 A.M. towboat alongside and at 10 A.M. moored off Shanghai |
| Saturday, September 30 | Took in our first tea |
| Wednesday, November 1 | 4 P.M. took in our last box of tea and battened down |
| Thursday, November 2 | Hove up port anchor and hove short on starboard one |
| | 3:30 P.M. dropped a mile and a half down the river to a clear anchorage |
| Saturday, November 4 | 8:30 A.M. homeward bound! |
| | 8 P.M. anchored off Wuhsien |
| Sunday, November 5 | At sea once more |
| Tuesday, November 7 | 4 P.M. sighted Turnabout Island |
| Tuesday, November 14 | 2 P.M. sighted island of Great Natuna, extending from Lat. 3°40′ to 4°16′ N, and from Long. 108°11′ to 108°26′ E |
| Thursday, November 16 | Tambelan Islands in sight, extending from Lat. 7′ to 2°15′ N and from Long. 105° 32′ to 108°32′ E |
| Friday, November 17 | 3 A.M. crossed the Line in Long. 107° E |
| Sunday, November 19 | Twenty islands in sight in Gaspar Strait, anchored several times |
| Wednesday, November 22 | Passed thro' Clements Strait, between Bangka and Billiton islands |
| Thursday, November 23 | Daylight, Islands of Two Brothers in sight |
| | 9 A.M. Sumatra |
| | 11 A.M. Java in plain sight |
| | 2 P.M. passed between the Button and Java and hove to off Anjer |
| | 8 P.M. passed Java Head in Lat. 6°48′ S, Long. 105°13′ E, and entered the Indian Ocean |

1855

| Saturday, January 27 | George Hall, son of one of our passengers, died at daylight |
| Wednesday, February 14 | Took a pilot |

End

# Glossary

ABACK  when the wind is on the forward side of the sails, forcing them against the masts and driving the vessel astern

BACKSTAY  a rope or stay, part of a ship's standing rigging, leading from the upper part of any mast above a lowermast to each side of the ship and fastened to a chain plate

BEAM  the greatest breadth of a vessel

BELL  a half-hour period of watch indicated by the strokes of a bell

BEND SAIL  to secure a sail to its proper yard or boom

BITTS  stout posts of wood or iron mounted on the deck of a ship and around which mooring or towing lines are made fast

BLOCK  a device consisting of a frame or shell in which there are one or more sheaves, or rollers, over which ropes are run

BOBSTAYS  chains or wire cables, part of a ship's standing rigging, extending from the end of the bowsprit to chain plates in the vessel's stem

BOOM  a spar used to spread the foot of a fore-and-aft sail

BOWSPRIT  a heavy spar projecting from a sailing vessel's stem, a chief support of the foremast by stays, and that from which the headsails are set

BRACE  one of the ropes which control the horizontal motion of a yard; to haul (a yard) around by means of a brace

BRACE PENDANT  a length of chain or rope, one end fastened to the yard and the other spliced into the brace block

BRAIL  one of the ropes by which loose-footed gaffsails, such as spencers, are gathered in to the mast for furling; to take in by the brails

BREAST BACKSTAY  an extra support to a topmast consisting of a rope extending from topmast head on the weather side to the channels forward of the standing backstays

BUNT  middle part of a square sail that lies on top of the yard when the sail is furled

BUNTLINE  one of the lines attached to the foot of a square sail to gather a sail up to its yard or to spill it

CAPSTAN   a mechanical shipboard device used in hoisting yards, heaving in anchors, and doing other heavy chores

CAT THE ANCHOR   to heave the ring of an anchor to the cathead, a heavy timber projecting from either bow of a sailing ship

CHANNELS   flat ledges of wood projecting outboard from the ship's sides to give greater spread to the lower rigging

CHIPS   ship's carpenter

CLEW   a lower corner of a square sail or after corner of a fore-and-aft sail; to haul (a sail) up or down by ropes through the clews

COCKBILLED ANCHOR   an anchor hanging over a ship's bow, secured by a stopper, and ready to be released

COPPER   sheets of copper sheathing to protect the bottom exterior of a wooden ship against marine worms and the growth of fouling organisms

COURSE   a sail bent to one of the lowest yards of a square-rigged ship

CROSS   to hoist from the deck and place in a horizontal position a yard on a mast of a square-rigged ship

CROSSJACK   a square sail set on the lowest yard of the mizzen mast of a full-rigged ship

CROSSTREES   two pieces of timber placed athwartship across trestletrees, supporting the top or platform at the lower masthead and spreading the shrouds

DOGWATCH   a two-hour watch on board ship, from 4 to 6 or 6 to 8 P.M., which permits a shift in the order of the watches every twenty-four hours so that the same men will not have the same watch every night

DOLDRUMS   a belt of calms and light airs lying between the trade winds of the Northern and Southern hemispheres

DUFF   a mixture of flour and water with raisins added. A sea tradition is to serve this dish on Thursdays

EARING   a short piece of rope used to secure a corner of a sail in position on a yard

EYES OF RIGGING   loops or bights at the upper end of the shrouds, around a masthead

FLEET   to free or loosen the blocks of a tackle after they have been drawn together

FLEMISH COIL   the method of spirally coiling a rope flat on deck so that all the turns lie snugly

FOOTROPE   a heavily served stout rope extending along and suspended from a yard, on which men stand when reefing, furling, bending, or un-bending a sail

FORE BOWLINE   a rope used to stretch forward a square foresail's weather leech when sailing close-hauled

FORECASTLE   the forward living compartment of a ship's crew, or that part of a vessel's upper deck forward of the foremast

FORESAIL   a sail carried on the foreyard and the lowest sail on the foremast

FORESTAY   a stay leading from the foremast head to the deck and from which the fore-topmast staysail is set

FOXES   strands formed by twisting several yarns of rope together

FULL AND BY   when a ship is sailing close to the wind but is keeping its sails full

FURL   to roll a sail up to its yard and fasten it with a gasket

GAFF   a spar that hoists a fore-and-aft sail abaft the mast and upon which the head of the sail is extended

GASKET   a small line or band of canvas used to make sails fast to yards or booms

GIG   a light ship's boat propelled by oars or sails

GIN   a block with a single sheave of large diameter

GO ABOUT   to turn a ship's bow and proceed on the other tack

GREASE DOWN   to apply a lubricant, or "slush," to a mast as a preservative, or along the course of a yard parrel to prevent friction

GULFWEED   a branching yellow weed with berrylike air vessels, great quantities of which are found floating in the Sargasso Sea and the Gulf Stream

GUNWALE   the uppermost planking of a ship's side

GYPSYHEAD   the drum of a winch around which a rope or cable is turned for heaving in or for raising a sail or a yard

HALYARD   a rope for hoisting and lowering yards, gaffs, and sails

HAWSER   a large rope for towing, mooring, or securing a ship

HEAVE THE LEAD   to use the lead to determine the water's depth

HEAVE TO   to bring a square-rigged sailing vessel under reduced sail area close to the wind by bracing the yards and to adjust the steering wheel so that the vessel will make minimal headway and will drift to leeward for easier riding; to back the mainyards in order to check a vessel's way in picking up a pilot

HOLYSTONE   to scrub a ship's wooden deck with soft white sandstone and loose sand and water

HORN   Cape Horn, at the southern extremity of South America

JACK AT THE FORE   the flag consisting of the union of the American ensign (jack) when flown at the foremast to signal the need for a pilot

JIB   a triangular sail set upon a stay extending from the bowsprit and jib-boom upward to the foremast

JIB GUY   a rope, cable, or chain for laterally staying the jibboom

KID   a shallow tub or pan in which a seaman's food is served

LANYARD   a rope rove through the deadeyes and used to set up the rigging

LARBOARD   an old term for the left, or port, side of a ship

LEAD   a heavy, cylindrical piece of lead with a recess in the bottom in which tallow is placed to pick up a sample of the sea's bottom. A line is attached to its top for casting the lead over the side to determine the water's depth

LEE   away from the wind

LEECH   either vertical edge of a square sail

LEEWAY   amount of drift a vessel is carried to leeward by force of the wind

LIFT   a cable or chain extending from the mast to each end of a yard for taking the weight of a yard so that it can be topped to the desired angle

LINE   the Equator. It is tradition that a seaman be subjected to an initiation ritual the first time he crosses the Line, thereby becoming a "shellback"

LOG   a device for measuring the speed of a vessel through the water

MAINSAIL   the sail bent to the main yard

MAN IN CHAINS   a seaman standing on a narrow platform, or channel, out to which the fore chain plates project, and on which he is in a good position to take soundings, or measure the depth of the water with a sounding lead

OCTANT   a navigating instrument, with an arc of 45°, for measuring the altitude of celestial bodies

OUTRIGGER   an extension bolted to each side of the crosstrees to spread backstays

PEAK HALYARDS   the ropes which hoist the peak, or after, end of a gaff

POOP DECK   the deck abaft the mizzen mast

PORT   the left side of a vessel when facing forward

PREVENTER STAY   an additional rope or wire placed alongside an overburdened brace or backstay to relieve pressure

PROA   an undecked Indonesian boat propelled by sails, oars, or paddles

QUARTER   the upper portion of the ship's sides near the stern

QUARTER BOAT   a small boat suspended from davits at the ship's quarter

RANGE   a specified length of anchor cable

RATLINE   a short length of small line seized and clove-hitched across the shrouds, acting as a round of a ladder for seamen to use when ascending or descending from aloft

RATTLE DOWN   to fit new ratlines to the shrouds

REEF   a part of a sail taken in or let out in regulating size; to reduce sail area by folding up part of it and securing it by tying reef points (pieces of small rope) around that portion

REEF JIG   a small tackle used in reefing sails to stretch taut the reefing band (a strip of canvas across a sail which takes the stress off the reef points before those points are made fast)

REEF TACKLE   a small purchase to facilitate the reefing of a heavy sail

REEVE   to pass a line or rope through an opening in a block, deadeye, cleat, thimble, ringbolt, or similar device

RING STOPPER   a short length of chain used to secure the ring of an anchor

ROYAL   the square sail above the topgallant sail

SCOUSE   a sailor's dish made of stewed preserved vegetables and sea biscuits

SCUPPERS   drains from the deck waterways

SENNIT   small cordage made by braiding rope yarns

SERVE   to wind or bind a rope or cable tightly with spun yarn or marline

SET UP   to take up slack in the stays and shrouds with a tackle

SHANK PAINTER   the chain holding the fluke of an anchor to the ship's rail or the steel plate by the cathead

SHEAVE   a wooden or metal grooved wheel rotating upon a pin in a block, yard, or mast, over which a rope is run

SHEET   a rope or chain that regulates the angle at which a sail is set in relation to the wind

SHEET HOME   to pull or haul on a sheet until the foot of the sail is as straight and tight as possible

SHROUD   a heavy rope or wire cable fitted over a masthead and extending to a vessel's side to support a mast laterally

SKYSAIL   a small square sail set above the royal

SLUSH DOWN.   See GREASE DOWN

SOUNDINGS  a place at sea where bottom can be reached with the deep-sea lead, ninety to one hundred and twenty fathoms in length

SPANKER  the gaffsail set abaft the mizzen mast

SPAR  general term for a mast, yard, boom, gaff, or bowsprit

SPENCER  a trapezoidal gaffsail without a boom, set abaft the fore or main lower masts of a ship or bark

SPOUTER  a whale ship

SQUILGEE  a hoelike implement with a rubber edge used to scrape water off wet decks

STARBOARD  the right side of a ship when facing forward

STAY  a rope or cable in a ship's standing rigging for supporting and stiffening a mast, leading from the head of one mast down to another or to the deck

STAYSAIL  a triangular or trapezoidal fore-and-aft sail hoisted on a stay

STREAM CHAIN  a close-linked chain used with the stream anchor (a light anchor used at the stern, in conjunction with a bow anchor, to prevent a ship from swinging)

STUDDING SAIL  a light square sail set on portable extensions of yardarms and used in fair winds

TACK  the lower, forward corner of a fore-and-aft sail; the rope holding down the lower, forward corner of a course; the weather clew of a course; the direction of a ship with respect to the trim of her sails; to change the direction of (a sailing ship) by turning the bow to the wind

TACKLE  a ship's rigging; a network of ropes or wires rove through blocks and over sheaves to afford a mechanical assistance in lifting or controlling an object of weight or force

TAR DOWN  to coat standing rigging with tar, or with a mixture containing tar, as a preservative

TOP  a platform supported by the trestletrees of a mast and serving as a spreader for topmast rigging

TOPGALLANT SAIL  the square sail above the topsail

TOPPING LIFT  a tackle by which the after, or outer, end of a boom is hoisted or supported

TOPSAIL  the square sail above the course or crossjack

TRADE WINDS  winds that blow from a relatively constant direction

TRYSAIL MAST  small mast abaft the fore and main lower masts on which are hoisted the spencers

T<small>URN IN</small>   to secure a shroud or backstay by passing the end around and fastening it to its standing part

V<small>ANG</small>   a pendant with tackle at its lower end leading from the peak, or after, end of a gaff to the deck at a vessel's side to steady the gaff

V<small>ITRIOL</small>   sulfuric acid

W<small>EAR SHIP</small>   to bring a sailing ship on another tack by putting the helm up and turning the stern to the wind; opposite of to tack

W<small>EATHER</small>   toward the wind

W<small>EATHER CLOTH</small>   a canvas or tarpaulin shelter placed in the weather rigging of a sailing vessel as a protection against rain, wind, and spray

W<small>EIGH ANCHOR</small>   to raise or heave in the anchor

W<small>HIP BLOCK</small>   a single block with a rope rove through it

W<small>INDLASS</small>   a mechanism for heaving in the anchor, usually mounted on the forecastlehead of a sailing ship

Y<small>ARD</small>   a long spar suspended horizontally to the forward side of a mast and to which the head of a square sail is bent

# Index